Overwhelmed

And other words you
give your power away too.

Karen Jackson

Soul Evolution Publishing

ISBN: 978-1-3999-2683-6

DEDICATION

To my family unit, I love you. Thank you for your unconditional love and acceptance of my uniqueness, for letting me be loved and free at the same time, thank you for trusting in the flow of life that I follow. Thank you for not ever feeling the need to clip my wings. You are my world.

A special thank you to my daughter Isabelle (Izzy) for patiently proofreading this book, to my son Finley, for asking me every day how I am going with the book, and to my bloke, you are my rock, I love you. I am so grateful to you all for choosing me.

To all my ancestors who have walked the path before me, to all the souls who had their power taken away by force, I honour you. I speak the words for you, I honour my privilege in this lifetime and dedicate my suffering in this earth walk to aid the expansion and evolution of the souls who are ready to read these words.

To my guides, to the energies of the directions, to mother earth, father sky, grandmother moon, grandfather fire, thank you for always holding a space for my soul and my growth, I honour you.

To my sisters whom I have met in this lifetime, thank you. You have helped me heal the sister wound. The wound of the feminine that I could feel in my psyche. I am blessed that there are so many of you, I honour you all.

To my teachers, mentors and guides in this lifetime, thank you for always holding the space and challenging me to grow.

CONTENTS

CHAPTER ONE
LET'S BEGIN

Words have always been magical for me. I feel their power physically, their energy vibrating in my cells. When someone says something beautiful to me, I feel my heart centre respond. When someone says something hurtful, or loaded with negative energy, I feel like I have been punched in the stomach.

I was so amazed when I learnt that we are vibrational beings, that nothing in our lives is actually 'solid'. Our physical world that we inhabit is made up of atoms, vibrating close to each other but not physically touching. This is science, it has been proven. Therefore, we are comprised of more space (between the atoms), than we are the atoms themselves. It feels that our whole society focuses on the seen, what appears to be 'real'. (I will include a note about quantum physics, that explains this a little bit more at the end of this chapter.)

I love to inquire, to look deeper…

What about all that space?

What about the unseen?

I am a truth-seeker and a change-maker. I don't ever expect to come up with answers to the many questions that I have. I just love to discover, to experience, to grow, and with each inquiry to free myself a little bit more. To step further into the purpose of my soul.

I have suffered a lot during this incarnation on earth. As have you, as has your neighbour. We all do. It is the nature of being human. This is how our souls evolve.

The wake up call for me, was after I was ignoring the gentle nudges of the universe trying to get me back on my path. I was trapped in low self worth, not wanting to be seen, not believing that I was here for anything special, not really even knowing who I was.

I was totally and utterly lost.

Does it resonate with you, if I say that I knew there was something inside of me? I knew deep down that I mattered? But, I didn't know what it was, and most importantly, I didn't quite believe it?

I began to believe over time. To remember the power inside of me. The Universe sent me some lessons to help me remember, to help me find my way back to my soul. Some of the lessons for my soul's growth came in the form of breast cancer. Not once, but twice.

During this time, I started to look at my thoughts. I leant into the belief that I create my reality. I took radical responsibility for myself. I started to look after all of me, to lead myself. I began to heal the layers of all the limiting beliefs in my head. I took care of my physical body. I honoured my boundaries. I started saying 'No" to the things that I didn't want to do. I gave myself permission to see less of the people that I didn't want to see.

I started to reserve my energy and my mental capacity

for the things and people that lit me up. My energy and wellness became my priority. Without it, I couldn't be there for my family. I finally got it. I became focused on soul and energetic expansion. On vibrating at a higher level. I stopped trying to control everything and everyone. I accepted people where they were and let them take responsibility for themselves. Most importantly, I completely surrendered.

I let go.

I let go of the grasping of life, and I trusted. I spent my time since the second diagnosis remembering who I am, as I didn't quite get it the first time.

I observed all the mindset beliefs, both of my own making and from society, that bound tightly around my soul. They were running through my body, causing constriction. These false limits that in each moment, were leading me further away from joy, from my purpose, from my belief and trust in myself.

I set the intention to unbind myself from them, slowly and steadily. One by one, I noticed them. I loved them. I loved the version of me that had believed them. I gave them the space to be healed. I decided to either walk with them woven into my life, but not taking my power away (fear). Or to let them go completely.

With my own healing, belief in myself, the universe and acknowledgment that I have something to offer the world, I now share my unique blend of wisdom with my clients, students and community. I do this by life, business and spiritual coaching, teaching yoga and how to use essential oils, human design, abstract art, writing and more.

In my work, I witnessed the same words being repeated over and over again. I noticed these words, because I know them very well. These words are the ones that I used to say and believe.

I know it didn't feel good saying and believing all of those things. In these pages, I share the internal questioning, discovery and embodiment that helped me get to the other side of that limiting low vibrational energy.

It lights me up to see the same energy loops that are woven into the lives and beings of my students, clients and soulpreneur (1) sisters, being released and transformed into belief and personal power, by looking at these words and reframing them.

As a lover of words, and knowing that they create our reality, some words jump out at me. When I hear certain words (the chapter titles), I get downloads and messages. Sometimes I feel intense rage, or I feel like I can't breathe. I can feel the physical constriction it has energetically put upon us all. I feel the rage of the ancestors, of those who have come before us. I feel the energy of oppression, the energy of not enough-ness. The energy of supposed power of one over the other, of force, hierarchy, division, polarity, them and us.

I don't like it. I don't think any of us do at soul level, the oppressor or the oppressed.

My soul literally screams inside of my body. It feels so intense and emotional. Now, I can notice them, I am able to allow the associated emotions to flow out of me so that they no longer effect my energy. I do this by writing, creating a podcast episode, creating a yoga lesson plan, and sometimes I dance and shake them out.

The phrase that inspired me to write this book, came from hearing on a daily basis the souls around me saying…

" I am so overwhelmed."

Each time I heard that word, it shook me. I could see so clearly how it takes the power away from the person saying it. I observed how that phrase stopped them taking aligned action in their lives. It was draining their personal power.

My intention for you as a reader, is to trust that you have this book in your hands for a reason. To be present with these pages. Maybe make a lovely comforting drink, sit somewhere peaceful, make sure you won't be disturbed and really be with me, the book, and most importantly with yourself.

Let the words penetrate your aura, let them, swirl around your head, let them trigger you, let some of them soothe you, let some of them shake you. Become an observer of how your body feels or responds to certain words and phrases that are on the page in front of you.

In the times when something feels like a barb. Stop. Take a pause. Allow yourself to feel and reflect. This is where the potential for healing and growth is. Use this time here, to reconnect to your feelings. Allow the emotions that you may have suppressed beneath the words that you use to hide behind, to surface.

You … beautiful soul are a spiritual being, in a body, with emotions. You are here to feel it all.

My wish for this book, is that it will be instrumental in helping you to move into your own healing a little bit more. That it will inspire you to step into your power a little bit more. As you heal and hold more compassion for yourself, perhaps you can extend this compassion and acceptance to others. If we all did this work, I believe, there would be a chance of more harmony and kindness on this planet.

If this is all new to you, I hope that it opens a door to a wonderful inner scape of your own light, and helps you to remember that you matter and are so needed in this World.

At the end of the chapters, I have included some of my poetry. A few years ago, poetry started to flow through me, often a random and unexpected stream of words, and has become a part of my own healing. I feel called to share them with you, as I wish that some of the words might aid your own healing and transformation.

Written with so much love K xxx

A note on quantum physics as promised.

I will keep this very high level, as it is such an in depth topic and I am not an expert. But quantum physics makes so much sense to me and has shaped how I live now. The world that we live in, that your body inhabits, is known as the 3D world. The quantum field is the 5D, it is full of limitless possibilities that our brain cannot even comprehend. We have the power to manifest our dreams from the quantum field into our physical reality, depending on what we focus upon and what we believe. Quantum physicists have discovered that the things that appear 'real' and 'solid' in our everyday lives aren't. They are atoms vibrating at different frequencies and between each atom is space, they aren't physically touching. Nothing in our world is physically solid, not even our own bodies. We are vibrational, energetic beings. Vibrational frequency is known to effect this space in between. Music, thoughts, emotions, actions, they all carry vibrational frequency, and affect everything.

Now this part blows my mind, quantum scientists are able to measure a quantum particle in two ways, they can measure its movement or its location. But, they can't measure both at the same time. What they found was that the quantum particles always show up where the physicist believes that it will appear. So two physicists will have the particles showing up in different locations. As I discuss in the chapter on failure later, each of us has a different lens of perception and expectations, so the particles will show up differently for each and every one of us in the world. This is how powerful we are, and how limited we can be when we don't open ourselves up to our limitless possibility. Please investigate all of this yourself if interests you. I am not a quantum expert and am only explaining my understanding of it.

ot know where you are right

You might feel lost

But I can see you

I can feel you

I can glimpse you, in the moments when
your eye's sparkle

Radiating the power of that light that is
inside of you

That has always been inside of you

And always will be

I will hold the space until you can see it
yourself

I will keep re-finding my own light

Time and time again

As the old patterns keep surfacing

As the old limits keep tightening around my
soul

One by one

Patiently

I will keep rediscovering me

The me underneath it all

I will keep unbinding the limits that encircle
me

It is time to become UNBOUND

CHAPTER TWO
HOW TO USE THIS BOOK

I wanted to add some layers to this book, so that you could take your own journey with it, to whatever level is right for you. For it to be a space to come back to and reflect upon. A space for you to reconnect with yourself, to heal and to power up

I have created a separate workbook that you can download by visiting this link, and the option to have an additional gift from me. https://www.iamkarenjackson.co.uk/overwhlemed-workbook

This will be a space to contemplate a set of prompts for your self inquiry, contained within the chapters. Alternatively, I recommend having a journal to record your thoughts.

As I write this book, I honour it as a collaboration with the universe. I believe that everything we co-create has its own energy, and is a creative entity, with its own essence. The energy of this book feels like it is inviting us all to slow down, to be with it for a little while. For it to feel like an inquisitive, caring friend, who sees your light and power, who believes in you, and holds you, as you gently unravel that which binds you.

I wish for if to feel like a conversation from my soul to your soul.

I will invite you at certain parts of the book to take a pause. Our world is so pressurised and hurried, we are constantly stimulated with little time to practice applying the knowledge that we learn.

Do you believe that less is more? That embodying what we are learning matters more than how much we 'know'?

If you do, please take me up on the invitations scattered through the pages, for you to have a play with the sacred pause. With creating space. See how it feels in your nervous system.

Does it feel blissful to stop, or does it feel uncomfortable?

I have created space for you to record your a-ha's in your workbook or journal. Those moments when something just clicks into place, when you get a full body reaction, an indication that there is some magic and medicine there for your soul, a space to note what your body identifies as important for you at this time.

In the workbook, is a space for you to record the beliefs that you don't want to believe, or to limit you anymore. There is a pretty good chance that they are not yours anyway. And space for my favourite, a Joy list, as you remember the things that light you up, you can make a list and commit to doing more of these.

Sending you so much love, I am so happy to walk beside you.

PS: We begin on the next page. The Soul Contract is a hangover from my law degree! Intention setting matters, the brain doesn't know that it's not a real contract. When you allow yourself to dream and to wish, the brain goes there, as if what you have written has manifested and is part of your life. When you set an intention with emotion and belief, something changes. Are you excited to start the change now? To begin to step further towards your future self? I am excited for you.

CHAPTER THREE
SOUL CONTRACT

I ……………………………..

Promise to listen to my body, emotions, energy and soul. To discover the words that I use to hide behind, and give my power away too. I am committed to learning how I really feel, and to creating space, so that I can discover and listen to my emotions.

I will be compassionate and non-judgemental with myself. I will love the version of me now, in full acceptance.

I will honour the version of me that will feel tender and stripped back, as I release layer after layer of conditioning.

I am ready to remember deep down that I matter, that I am enough, just as I am.

I am ready to step away from the ideals that have been passed down and pressed upon me.

I am ready to take my power back.

Date …………

Signed ………..

One more request please before you go any further….

As you read and absorb the words and medicine of the teachings, please remember, that there is absolutely no judgement from myself. I have been in all of this, felt through it all. It was too painful for my soul to stay in that energy. So I chose via my actions not to hang around with those words anymore. I felt called to stop hiding my light.

I still slip into all of what I have written about, because I am human, with a brain and an ego, this is what they do. When I notice, I smile, I choose to love myself even more. Then I slow my breath, I ground myself and I journey within again, to see how I am really doing.

When I began to see all the power that I was giving away to the beliefs in my mind, that often weren't even mine. I realised that I didn't even consider the possibility, that I could have more joy in my life. I chose to smother myself with compassion and understanding. I realised that I had been programmed and that was okay. This was deep self acceptance, it was challenging for me. That way of being had given me valuable experience, it had kept me safe.

No judgement and lashings of compassion.

CHAPTER FOUR
WARRIOR WOMAN

I remember it so vividly, laying in bed, curled up, sobbing, attempting desperately to make a deal with the higher powers. God. Universe. Source.

I pleaded, over and over again.

"If anyone is listening, please give me ten more years of living in this body, so that our children can remember me. So that I can pass on my wisdom, some of the things that I wish I would have known. Let me pass on my medicine, more of my heart. Let me have those awkward conversations about sex and smoking, let me ground them, let me have more cuddles on the sofa, more laughs, just more please. More."

My son Finley was 6 months old and my daughter Isabelle was 4 years old. I had just been diagnosed with breast cancer.

It felt like my whole being, my whole essence, was just swept up with big decisions, none of which I wanted to make.

I wanted it to all just go away.

I surrendered my body to being studied, injected, burned, sliced and rearranged, to save my life. Followed by ongoing emotional and body altering hormone treatment.

I lost all sense of myself.

I felt ethereal, like I wasn't really there. I felt like I was slowly leaving, wispy, it was hard for me to grab onto life. I didn't know what I thought, or what I was feeling. I was pretty numb.

At the same time as feeling like this, I had cast myself into the role of being a superhero. I donned my warrior woman persona, in an attempt to keep it altogether for everyone around me. It was an exhausting facade to wear, but it served its purpose, it was an amazing coping mechanism.

Unless we are living aligned with our own uniqueness, we have the tendency as humans to people please, to wear a facade. This is such a drain on our energy. Over time, the mask starts to get very heavy and oppressive. It takes effort and energy to keep putting the mask on day after day.

Healing can also be very tiring and extremely uncomfortable. But the amount of energy, resentment, frustration, bitterness and inner turmoil you save from wearing that mask of inauthenticity, is invaluable.

It is where life is.

As warrior woman, I was able to go through the motions, I looked so strong. All the pain appeared to be hitting me and rolling off my tough outer exterior. On the outside it looked as though I was able to cope with anything. My ego was falsely boosted by the praise I was getting. Being told over and over again how strong I was.

You see, when the pain, fear, and emotions that I was placed in front of bounced off my tough exterior, I was denying them. I wasn't processing them.

In this place of avoidance, the words I used to hide behind, were like a safety blanket, hiding the reality of what I was really feeling.

I didn't want to look.

I was scared.

The badges of honour that society congratulated me for, I collected with relish. I had a badge for 'being strong,' another for 'getting on with it.' There were many more. My ego soaked them all up, basking in the glory of the praise I was receiving. After cancer treatment, this all went away. I was left asking myself, who am I now? Who is warrior woman now? If she is gone and I don't have anything to fight, who am I?

I fell into the void.

Over a period of time, I chose to let go of that title. I let go of the label that I was adorned with. In order to do that, I had to open up to vulnerability which was a challenge for me. I was surprised to learn that I believed at a subconscious level that being vulnerable was weak. I started to inquire and it all began to make sense.

I so wanted to be strong, the strong survived, didn't they? I had to be strong to survive cancer. Thats what I had learnt, but, I knew deep in my heart, that this wasn't the truth. I started to explore, so that I could free myself of this limited way of thinking.

Over time, I reprogrammed my belief that vulnerability was weakness. I realised that vulnerability requires strength, beauty, humanness, and realness. I started to open myself up. I surrendered wonder woman, so that I could access the raw and tender emotions inside of me that had been ignored. I allowed the energy to begin to circulate through my body. It hurt. At times, it took my breath away, it stung my eyes. Always momentarily, then it passed.

During the healing process, it was wave after wave of emotions hitting me so hard one moment and then soothing me in the next. The sweetness of relief, was like the calm after the storm, the beautiful cleansing smell after the rain. I was cleansing my internal beliefs and the stagnation of emotions and energy that had collected in every corner of my being.

I was fully embodying what I was teaching in Yoga, that thoughts and emotions change every minute. They come and they go. I observed them. I accepted them all. I felt them all. I shone a light on them all, in order for them to be seen and acknowledged. So that they could be free to move through me and not take up residence anymore.

I finally honoured myself and gave myself the space and softness to heal.

Warrior woman served me so well at the time though, I have no regrets. She enabled me to not go to pieces in front of our children. Her martyrdom to her own feelings helped me to be able to cocoon them. I didn't want their childhood to be focused on mummy's cancer.

I remember doing the school run when I was first diagnosed, luckily it was summer and I could let the tears flow behind my sunglasses, so that I could "Put on a brave face" and "Get on with it." These phrases, were part of the fabric of society and times that I grew up in, they programmed me well. The programming was so strong, that it was my automatic reaction to put on those masks as soon as I was diagnosed. Not to connect with my emotions.

I remember vividly the moment that I received the initial diagnosis. It felt like I was an observer, like I had detached my soul from my body and emotions. I was floating opposite to myself. I can see it, and remember it so clearly.

In my minds eye, I can see the shock on my face, the gasp of my breath. I can feel the panic and restriction in my throat and my stomach. I can see the big gulp that I took, forcing down the natural compulsion to sob. The second after this initial reaction, I see myself leaning forward, hands on my lap. Fierce eyes, determined eyes, asking straight away, about the action plan. What do I need to do, what are my options?

I did not give myself any time to feel, or to process.

Let's get to it. Let's get into action.

I felt like I was suffocating, like my soul was being submerged by the different intense and painful thoughts, emotions and feelings that I was pushing away. I knew it felt chaotic. I knew it felt too much. I was scared that I couldn't really cope. I knew I was struggling to breathe. I wanted to run away. It felt like a tsunami of 'whelm' was covering me. I just wanted to hide from it all. Safely tucked out of sight until it had passed. My ego wanted to go straight into flight mode, my heart was in fight.

It did pass though. Like life, like all emotions, they pass. All feelings change, each moment moves on to another moment. The problem for me, and so many of my students and clients is, that if we don't honour the emotions, acknowledge them, see them and feel them, they stick around. They invade and hijack our energetic and nervous systems. In doing so, they steer us away from our true nature and our inner peace.

Since then, I have been on a personal quest to heal myself on every level possible, emotional, physical, energetic and spiritual. To discover what was underneath these emotions.

I found it.

I was terrified of death. I wasn't accepting that it was a natural part of life. So I chose to surrender. I faced the fact that I would die. At some level, I got to be okay with that.

My ego created resistance to death, but my soul needed the peace that acceptance brings. I fully felt into and trusted, that when my physical body dies, my soul, which is pure energy will go home, back to the universal collective consciousness.

I learnt that energy is energy and never disappears, it just changes form. I trusted that if I did leave our children early, it was all part of the plan. So I let go.

As I let go, I let go of the pain I had created by holding on so tightly. The cramp like constriction this grasping caused throughout me, could soften.

It was blissful.

Alongside this, I remembered that I am powerful, that what I do matters, that my thoughts matter. I dedicated myself to discovering, unwinding and unbinding one limiting belief at a time, that was no longer serving me. I started to see them and let them go. Most of them weren't even mine anyway. They were old programs, created by our ancestors, as a survival mechanism. Curated by society and people in power to keep the masses compliant, to encourage us to forget our true worth and value.

They were just not working for me anymore.

I have delighted, and still do, in being triggered.

Investigating each thought, my ways of coping, all the ways that society has trained me to keep going. With each discovery, I began to see what I had buried. I saw, honoured and felt into the emotions that I had ignored.

My soul started to crave feeling again. I wanted to feel, to feel it all, the joy and the pain. Feeling meant that I was alive. I love the feeling of being alive, with all its different facets, the light, the shadows, the joy and the pain.

I saw the irony in the fact that, the four years between my first and second cancer diagnosis, I wasn't living. I didn't realise it at the time. I had lost touch with myself.

Society would say I was overwhelmed.

I never said that word, even at the time. I just knew that I didn't feel good and that I didn't want to exist like this.

Allow me to take you with me through some of my self discovery and healing journey. In sharing this, I hope that it becomes the start of your own personal journey. A journey to reclaim your sovereignty, to take back your personal power, to deepen your awareness, to begin to honour all parts of yourself and all of your feelings.

A journey 'out of the whelm' to the other side, where life is.

Don't talk about it

Shhhhh don't talk about death

No-one mention that word to her
If we speak about it, it might happen
Let's pretend that everything is okay
That everything will be okay
Let's try and avoid it
Just don't mention it

Is that a luxury or is it a prison?

You see, the truth set me free
To face my mortality head on
To feel the pain of clinging on so tightly
The anxiety, the grasping energy
Hurt more than the letting go
Sweet surrender set me free

I am going to die

In the facing of it
I found joy
I chose to live
I chose to appreciate every sweet second
The pain, the beauty

I chose to feel it at all

CHAPTER FIVE
OVERWHELMED

Do you believe that language is important?

Do you believe, that the words you use, and the thoughts that you have matter?

An invitation to take a sacred pause, to contemplate the questions above. Get a drink, maybe look at the sky, meditate and then contemplate. Perhaps you will be called to get your journal, maybe have a discussion with someone you love. The more you practise weaving a beautiful little pause into your life, here and there, the more you soothe your nervous system. As you learn to slow down, you will come back home to your body, back home to you.

Whilst you take this time, I want to remind you, that you matter, that you're beautiful uniqueness is needed in this world. This won't be the only time that I say this. I believe in the power of repetition. I know that for myself, I might have heard the same message 77 times before I really hear it. Before I am ready to transform and embody the energy of that teaching, that has been falling on deaf ears for so long. I believe that we hear the words when we are ready to grow.

The words you choose to use, shapes the way that you express how you are feeling, and how you want to feel. Your words and thoughts create an energetic manifestation into the world. They also deeply effect the health of your cells, how your DNA is expressed and how others experience you.

Let's dive in now, the reason for this book, one of the words that makes me shiver when I hear it. Let's investigate the word overwhelm.

What is 'WHELM'? Can you really, truly be overwhelmed?

I typed this question in to the search engine… "Can you feel whelmed?"

These are the results I found. Overwhelm and underwhelm come from the older word 'whelm.'(2)To submerge; engulf, to overcome utterly; overwhelm, whelmed by misfortune, to roll or surge over something, as in becoming submerged. To engulf, submerge, or bury. A swimmer whelmed in a raging storm, to well up or flow. The brook whelmed up from its source. (3)

The same words kept coming up in the searches. References to water, being flooded, or buried under earth, engulfed, overloaded, saturated, clogged, burdened.

This made more sense, but, before we start to go deeper, let's look at one of the official definitions (3) of overwhelm. 'To cause someone to feel sudden strong emotion, they were overwhelmed by grief. If water overwhelms a place, it covers it suddenly and completely. The rain that caused the flooding was of such unusual intensity that the sewers were overwhelmed.'

Before I looked up the definitions, what felt so unsettling in my observations of souls around me using the word overwhelm, was the lack of emotional awareness that comes with the use of it. It was like a big cover up to hide the essence of what was really going on. Just like my warrior woman facade hid how I was really feeling.

In the definition above, it states specifically the emotion that the person was overwhelmed with, they were feeling so much grief. It recognises, identifies and pays homage to the actual feeling and emotion. We seem to have lost the true application of the word overwhelmed.

We miss out the messy emotional part.

The feeling part.

We just say we are overwhelmed.

But what are we really feeling?

In coaching sessions with a client, we start an inquiry to discover what is underneath any sense of 'whelm' that they are experiencing, so that we can start the healing process and move into aligned action or rest. Whatever their souls require.

Without awareness, we are operating blindly. We might not know who we are, or how we are projecting out into the world. We might not know what we are here for. We can become quite mindless, stuck in the everyday grind, the cycles and the paths that we think we should follow. When we operate from this state, we lose ourselves. I know for me, I did.

It was disorientating having so many different emotions swirling around, all unidentified, all unknown to me. Because I did not know what I was dealing with, I couldn't see the issues and emotions to understand them, to allow them to be reframed. My issues and limits stayed with me. Because they remained hidden, they weren't seen to be transformed. I felt the whelm, I felt suffocated but I didn't know what by, so I couldn't help myself.

Looking at the definitions and feeling into them, I found that its a sudden event, often intense, and this is where some of the problem lies. It feels like the right time to introduce emotions and yin yoga to you here.

I am a Yoga teacher and now specialise in teaching Yin. I believe Yin Yoga is one of the medicines that the world needs right now.

Yin Yoga works with the meridians and free flow of energy from the TCM (Traditional Chinese Medicine System). TCM advocates that emotions and a free flow of energy in the body are intertwined. We believe that there aren't any bad or good emotions. Emotions are simply a movement of energy. E-motion, energy in motion. Yet in society, we are taught that anger is negative, and often girls are programmed not to get angry. It's not attractive, it will scare people off. We have unspoken categories, woven into the fabric of our communities of acceptable emotions and ones that we should be more ashamed to feel. We even seem to have sub divisions and labels attaching certain emotions as being more acceptable to one gender or the other.

It does still feel to me, that the emotion of anger is more socially acceptable for men. As if it is almost expected. Females are subliminally taught to suppress our anger. So we don't look at it, we try and deny it, so it swirls around the body causing energetic imbalances that can go on to cause physical and emotional problems.

I have found in my own experience and in my coaching client's that there is a tendency to avoid expressing our anger to others. As women there is an undercurrent of being a 'good girl,' being 'accepted,' 'avoiding conflict,' 'not wanting to upset anyone,' or 'cause a problem.'

It is so saddening to see that both genders have been programmed what to feel and what not to feel.

Men, are told to 'man up,' 'don't cry like a girl'. They are encouraged to deny their own natural flow and release of energy and emotions. I believe that men are designed to cry too, because they have tear ducts and emotions. As far as I know, there isn't a specific design for a male eye. An eye is an eye, and it is designed to allow tears (energy, emotions) to leave the body. The release, that tears bring has been proven, you can learn more about the benefits of crying in the end notes. (5)

There are threads of out dated beliefs still circulating like the wind through society. Particularly the corporate world, no-one will take you seriously if you have feelings, if you show your emotions, if you cry. When you cry, you are weak, you are unstable. We can't have all that emotion in the workplace. We can't have that weakness.

Showing emotions, makes the emotionally repressed so uncomfortable, it is after all terribly messy isn't it? So much easier, if you just keep it all in.

It is everywhere, interwoven into the fabric of our society. So woven in that we can't always see the strands unless we start to look deeper. I wish that this inquiry will be the start of a deeper ongoing practise of discovery for you, both internally and externally.

In Yin Yoga, we sit with ourselves, and all of our emotions; current, repressed, and any that we anticipate into the future. We sit in shapes for minutes at a time, slowing the breath and simply allowing the emotions to move.

The same shape can feel like bliss one day, and torture the next, depending upon our emotions and what is going on in our lives. It is so sweet to surrender to the fact that it is all just a moving of energy. Our emotions are just moving energy. They aren't good or bad. One emotion isn't better or worse than the other. They just are.

Beautiful, beautiful acceptance of what is.

In Yin Yoga, we take away the drama, we know that we have emotions, and that they come and they go. We build up the discipline to let them move and to not attach excessive energy to them.

They come and they go.

Your emotions come and they go.

All your emotions are equally valid.

Yin is one of the most challenging practises that I have, and at the same time, it is one of the most liberating, and sometimes, one of the most blissful. It always brings me back to my body and away from the never ending swirling of my mind.

Intense emotions can be felt so strongly for about 90 seconds, after that, if allowed to be, they naturally begin to subside. We can get so scared of that feeling of intensity, that we panic and desperately try to suppress, to get away from that feeling, that emotion. Instead of letting the energy move, letting ourselves feel for a moment so that the energy can be dispersed, transformed and then released.

When the whelm moves in, we tend to build a dam, instead of letting the emotion pass. We add to our own discomfort.

Emotional intensity is a part of life, and it's a part of life that I love now. Both the pain and the joy. Because I am alive. I know it is part of this earth walk for my soul. I am here now to really truly live in lots of multifaceted ways. I want to feel it all. I am open and willing to feel my humanness.

I do not deny or attach any shame to any of the emotions that I feel. I hope by learning that all emotions are neutral, that they are simply moving energy, you can gift this to yourself. Your emotions are natural, valid, and nothing to be ashamed of beautiful soul.

The way towards healing, the way towards balance, is to allow yourself to feel, to be with that emotion and to let it pass. You can only heal, and understand what is under the whelm, if you know what you are actually feeling so that you can become aware of it, in order to let it go. If you deny yourself the awareness and the subsequent moving of that energy, that is when your energetic flow can get disrupted.

If your house is whelmed by water, it's useful to know that it is the medium of water, that you are dealing with. With water you could get a pump, or use a bucket to move the water. If you are whelmed by a landslide, it is the medium of earth that you are dealing with. You need different tools for each medium. Likewise, each emotion has a different flavour, a different texture and a different action to help you resolve it.

I know in my body, that I deal with the feeling of anger very differently to how I manage sadness, or joy.

Emotions are an indication of how we are really doing. For example, if you are whelmed by anger, there could be a boundary that keeps being crossed that you might need some conversations about. Or it could be that you are overworking yourself. Someone could be repeatedly disrespecting you, and you haven't found the self-worth or the words and belief yet, to speak up. So you feel angry. Or you might be so deeply sad. Knowing what the whelm is, the awareness of it, is essential.

In my own life and with my clients and students, I can't sort out overwhelm. But I can work through the feeling of anger and what is causing it. I can recognise and make changes if I am burning myself out. I can't, if I don't recognise it and just keep telling everyone how overwhelmed I am.

When a client comes to me, who hasn't worked with me before, I give them the space and ask the questions to help them shine a light to identify what they are really feeling. It might be one emotion and one situation, or several different ones, all at the same time. The relief on their faces is so beautiful. They have clarity, they can see, and they know that they can find a way through the feelings and situations now, because they can name it.

It becomes possible.

Their faces soften, their shoulders relax and their breath slows down. They feel seen and heard at a level they have been denying themselves. They are seen by myself, and most importantly, they have seen and heard themselves.

The most important person that you should listen to in your life, is you. Often we don't trust our inner voice. We have been taught to listen and rely upon external authorities, instead of connecting to the innate wisdom that resides inside of us.

We know that whelm means to submerge, but it doesn't just have to be what we deem to be negative, you can feel whelmed with joy. I know I have cried when everything just feels so wonderful and I am so full of joy and gratitude. I often cry with happiness, as it feels just as intense in my body as anger. The joy and the emotions, overspill as tears.

When I allow my emotions to move, I can feel the energy dissipate, this is the same for any emotion. Energy is energy, it doesn't disappear from existence, it moves.

In this world that we live in, we seem to have missed out the fact that underneath the overwhelm, is an emotion or a situation that we are whelmed by, that we are submerged under.

I don't believe that I can just say that I am overwhelmed, without the identification of the emotion. If I do, I am ignoring how I am really feeling. The question we should really be asking, is what are we feeling overwhelmed by?

I'd love to invite you to take a pause, and ponder, how is this resonating with you?

Do you feel anything in your body? Has what you have read so far given you any a-ha moments? Note down in the workbook, or your journal. Contemplation and embodiment is medicine.

Has anything changed for you? Anything that you deeply disagreed with?

I feel called to acknowledge, that I don't desire, or expect you to love everything that I write in this container, and definitely, not agree with me. In this space, I am expressing my perspective, my lived experience and observations. My own perspective could change in the space of the next second, tomorrow, or in ten years time. My perspective is not fixed, nothing is. I am open to seeing new things and forming new opinions. I am here to grow and learn from every experience and soul around me. We are all here to see the world differently, to have our own individual perspectives. That is how we evolve. You are here to be you, to be so beautifully unique. I am here to be me.

I have written this book to initiate inquiry, to spark the curiosity for you to find your own truth. For you to find the path to go deeper into your own healing and to remember your light.

Some questions to contemplate.

Is overwhelm at its core in our modern day lives, a feeling of too much?

If you feel overwhelmed, what is it that you are feeling or doing too much of?

What is really underneath it?

What are you feeling a lot of?

Without this understanding, you are continually hanging out in the energy of the emotions that you are feeling too much of, covering up, numbing out and moving yourself further away from inner peace, joy, ease and so much more goodness. If you can't identify how you are feeling, you delay the start of your journey to heal and grow.

It is far more convenient, tidier and neater, to just use

the word overwhelm instead of looking at our real feelings. Instead of softening, being vulnerable and letting those around us know how we are really feeling.

The way that I helped to heal myself and become more in touch with myself, to literally come back home to me, was self inquiry. The awareness of what I was truly thinking and believing. In essence, what you think and believe, informs your choices. Your choices, the moments, in life that you make one choice after the other, is your life.

If you believe that life is a series of choices that you make in each moment, and that you have the ability to choose, that makes you very powerful. Your thoughts, which influence the choices that you make matter.

When I truly felt this as a full body resonance, I submerged myself into investigating my own beliefs. Some were beautiful. Some were not. The ones that are not so beautiful, are called the shadows. But I realised, as I kept going, that nothing is as scary when we shine the light upon it.

The process that I use for my own growth and healing, mainly goes in this order, but it is not often linear. Healing, growth and life rarely is, sometimes it is as simple as that, often, not.

1. Inquiry
2. Awareness
3. Growth via aligned action
4. Embodiment
5. Transformation

This formula for me, leads to change. I know that change can feel like it might never happen, that it isn't possible, that you might feel stuck. When you start to shine the light of awareness, magic happens. It often becomes more challenging to stay in stagnation and ignorance, than it is to begin to gain awareness and take the aligned steps toward change and your souls growth.

As you shine the light of awareness, you start to see the potential path for your next aligned step, whether you leap, or whether you tentatively place one foot out at a time. You are moving. You are evolving.

As you keep moving, you get to play and practise. To try out your new beliefs, to see how they feel. Over time, you are able to shed the ones that don't feel so good anymore. As you discover how you want to feel, you are able to keep the beliefs that feel expansive. You become transformed and embody this new version of you with upgraded beliefs. When you acclimatise to this new version of you, if you choose your souls continued evolution, the time will come again to grow. Then if you desire more expansion and inner freedom, you repeat.

Over and over again.

One step at a time.

One layer at a time.

One thought pattern at a time.

One belief at a time.

Once you start to get used to change, you might feel more comfortable with it, and perhaps begin to seek it out, to strive to move towards your inner freedom each day. The changes can happen with more ease and speed each time you notice a block or a limiting belief. Your soul knows where to lead you, when you let it be heard.

I work with some beautiful souls, who speed through some of my courses, and then still talk to me about the problems that caused them to join in the first place. The souls who came with a busy head, read the sections and watched the videos about the busy head, and the next day tell me about the problems of their busy head. There was no aligned action taken. I want to remind you again that this is all said without judgement, I can only see because I have done it all myself, and still do sometimes.

Self love.

Self compassion.

Tenderness.

Aligned action.

Embodiment.

One step, one belief at a time.

Self inquiry and awareness can be a catalyst for you to start to see these toxic threads woven through the fabric of our world. Because we live in these societies, by default, they get entangled into our psyches. We get caught up in them. Over time, the more you practise, the more you begin to see them. You become able to catch them in your hand and unwind them from your body and soul, so that you can be free and can come back home to yourself.

Some questions for contemplation, to help you start to shine a light on what you truly think and feel. Be a kind, compassionate, objective investigator.

Do you believe that the words and thoughts of other people matter? If yes, is it true that your words and thoughts matter. If yes, what thought patterns do you feel called to start to let go of?

Are there any words you use towards yourself that are not loving and kind? If yes, which ones would you like to let go of?

Do you use the word overwhelm?

If yes, in what situations, do you use it?

Looking at the list, what emotions cause you to use the word overwhelm? What emotions, beliefs, thoughts or situations have triggered you to use that word?

What do you think is really going on, deep down?

Seeing these feelings and situations on paper, in black and white, what actions could you take to soften the feelings, to let them move, or to positively change the situations so that the same thing doesn't keep happening?

If there is anything else coming up for you, listen to yourself. Let the pen connect your heart to paper and keep writing.

Give yourself this time, space and attention.

In a loop

Exhausted
Round and round
In this loop

Comparison
Perfectionism
Fear on a loop

I can't see a way out

I am dizzy

CHAPTER SIX
TIME

Beautiful soul, have you ever considered how much of your power you give away to the concept of time?

It is such a challenge in this modern world, that is constantly asking us to do more, and go faster, to not give into the scarcity of time that surrounds us, 24/7.

Adverts continually bombard us with the message that more is more, encouraging us to find ways to fit more into an already overflowing lifestyle. I have realised that more doesn't feel like more to me, it feels like exhaustion. My soul feels fatigued. I am tired of being told what I need. My soul craves space. I desire less possessions in order to create more mental space in my head, and more physical space in my home. I wish for more space around the use of my time. I have way too many things. I am in the slow process of stripping it all back, of simplifying and it feels delicious.

For me, less is more, this feels like soul medicine, a return back to more simplicity.

With regards to our schedules, we will look at the concept of 'busy' in the next chapter, the two, time and busy are so intertwined.

Let's ignite some curiosity and awareness upon your relationship with time.

I'll begin by sharing my own personal story and

and reprogramming around time.

As I started to go through my mind, to see the filters that I had set in it, the limits that were binding me, the self created beliefs that were holding me back. I began to notice my own relationship with time. I am so grateful I did, because it was so obstructive, exhausting and soul destroying.

In a coaching training I was taking part in, I was invited to spend a few days checking in with my thoughts every hour, to see what I was actually thinking. My thoughts were, and still are complete chaos, that is the nature of the mind. That is why meditation is so helpful. However, I knew that the keys to my beliefs lay there. I love homework, so I did what was asked, and was absolutely amazed. The first day, was a day when I had things to do, that I had planned, but I was okay. There was no external pressure, or timelines that I had to meet, just the ones that I had set myself. It was at this point I started to look at myself with compassion and disbelief. I was so hard on myself. Such a demanding task master.

As I tuned in, I became aware of a string of words, whirring around my mind on repeat.

"I'm busy, I'm busy, I'm so busy"

I could feel these words creating an energetic sense of urgency, affecting my mind and body, stopping me from even sitting down, stopping me from preparing myself a nourishing meal, instead I was just grabbing bits to eat.

I was allowing this swirling whirlwind of energy to deny myself the rest, nourishment and care that my body needed. I observed myself diving headfirst from task to task. When I completed a task, I added more to my list, like a robot, must get this done, tick, add something else, tick and on it went.

WOW.

It really was a WOW moment for me, a massive a-ha. As I wasn't aware that it was there. I had after all, never really looked before. This is where I hope that you can hold the compassion for yourself and talk nicely to yourself.

We don't know what we don't know.

It is as simple as that. I could have chosen to berate myself. I didn't. I chose the path of love, of being curious, of being open.

What was I doing to myself? I was literally placing myself in a self imposed, never ending cycle of tasks, just because I was telling myself that I was busy.

My thoughts and beliefs, were creating my experience. I was constantly setting my nervous system into overdrive. I was wired.

I was amazed, and at the same time appalled that I was doing this to myself. That's when I decided that I really wanted to start to heal my relationship with time, and as always, with lashings and lashings of self compassion.

I took a deep breath, reset my energy, came back to my centre and I started to question it.

Is this actually true? Am I really this busy?

I sat with myself and my journal. I dedicated the pages to my healing, a space for me to get the whirring thoughts out of my head and onto paper. For me, it takes their power away. When I can see my thoughts in black and white, on paper, I can see clearly and a little more rationally. I can see them objectively, I can deal with them with more ease and less emotion.

So, I got my pen and paper out, and wrote the truth. In that moment, I felt my face soften. The feeling of the tension draining out of my body was visceral, my breath deepened and I felt peaceful.

I saw the lie. In that instant I saw the threads around us all, not just me, I zoomed out and saw us as a collective.

If we are busy, we are compliant, we don't have the time or the energy to question, to devote to ourselves, to start the journey of healing and self transformation. We are spending our time in the rat race, trying to be enough and have enough. As I type I have an image of a hamster in a wheel running mindlessly around and around, robotically perpetuating the cycle and the door to the cage is open. All they can see is the next task, the next little paw on the wheel and on it goes, unless they become aware and choose to stop.

My desire is that this book, this bundle of energy in your

hands or on your screen, acts like a stop sign, and you choose to jump off that wheel as soon as you can.

Where did these beliefs come from? Are they mine? They are in my head, but are they truly mine? I will share some questions for you to explore at the end of this chapter, if that feels good to you.

I could see the patterns that had been enforced on humans since industrialisation, clock in, clock out, define your day by hours, charge per hour, pay per hour, an hour of your time is worth this amount, mine is worth this. Our value being determined all by numbers. The measurement of our perceived value and worth calculated per the hours that we have worked.

I was directly linking my worth to the hours that I was working. Oh my goodness, and from a yoga teacher and coach no less. This is where my compassion for myself came in. I could have told myself off. I could have felt shame. I could have told myself that I should know better, that I was a rubbish yoga teacher, to have not been aware of this. I didn't. I used humour. I have a saying, "how beautifully human of me". I hold my hands over my heart and smile. I often laugh, with tenderness and complete acceptance. I am human. It is as simple as that. I am human, in this modern world, with a brain that gets programmed by all the messages, and I just got a bit carried away.

"How beautifully human of me."

I am pretty sure that I will get carried away, and

temporarily loose my centre again, time after time. The difference now, is that I tend to notice when I go off track. I can bring myself back, a little quicker each time, with a bit more ease, than at the start of my journey down into the rabbit hole of my mind.

Unconsciously, I was still in the old paradigm of believing that my worth was linked to a number, and that others got to determine my worth. Our whole society loves figures, like the money in the bank, the value of houses, clothes size, weight, wage.

How can we ever measure our brilliance and wellbeing, our joy, our memories, our experience, the things that really matter with a number?

My mind is flashing back to my 40th birthday, it was supposed to be a big celebration to mark 5 years of being cancer free, since my initial diagnosis. Being a pretty positive person, I had organised my own masked ball as a celebration of life and a chance to have all of my friends and family together, to thank them for their support and to celebrate being in each others lives. However, due to the circumstances, it felt like my own wake, but it was also very beautiful. The cancer had returned, and I was to go for surgery a few weeks later. That party, being with my loved ones, feeling their love directed towards me, was so special. No-one there cared at all what I earned. All we cared about was our human connection, and being there for each other. We were there in love and friendship. This is a powerful lesson to experience in this lifetime. I am pretty sure that no one actually cared about my 'numbers'. You cannot quantify human connection.

In our physical world we measure time in a linear way (this linear way, isn't real according to quantum physics). Linear time is man made. It is a concept, a system. I love learning from the deep wisdom engrained in ancient cultures, the ancient Greeks had two ways to view time. They named them Chronos and Kairos, which is so beautiful and to me makes so much sense.

Chronos is the linear concept of time, and it is so useful, it helps when we have to be somewhere by a certain time, it keeps the 3D world going in many ways. It helps us to honour each others energy and gives us a framework. That, in essence is what it is. A framework, a system, not something to give our power away too. It is a means of structuring logical linear steps to get somewhere, highly practical, highly useful. I embrace fully that I am a human and I thrive in lots of ways with structure, it helps bring order, but it is not a means with which I chose to prove my worth with anymore.

Kairos, on the other hand, refers to the quantum time. Deep time. The moments when you are in a magical place, with people you love, who light you up. It is the moment when your whole body naturally slows down. When your breath deepens. The moments when it feels like the linear time that we are so used to, is suspended. In these moments it is.

Time is a concept. A system that we all perceive differently, through our own lenses of perception, programming and belief systems.

We all have different experiences of time, and I know that in each moment, I personally experience time differently. Often when I am lost in a beautiful practise, or creative flow, I look at my watch and it feels like it 'should' be a lot later.

When I am in creation mode, I am completely in the moment, in joy, I am lost in it all. I want more, I wish it could keep going forever. It feels expansive. I feel expansive. It is such a beautiful way of being, just purely connected to the moment, and it is available to us all, with a little practice.

In these moments, I am experiencing life instead of hurriedly looking at my watch and moving step to hurried step.

As humans we are innately aware of our deep rooted feelings of 'not-enoughness', perpetuated, and enhanced by modern culture, if we allow it. It is part of the modern psyche. We are all judged so much, there is so much polarity, so much separation. So much being told by the powers that be, and each other, that this is good, this is bad, do this, don't do that. This results in comparison, perfectionism, and we start to not feel enough. We don't trust ourselves fully, we give our power away to others, or to the things that society values more than our beautiful humanness.

In order to heal my relationship with time, I had to heal my own self worth, the two healed beautifully together.

So how do we give our power away to time?

Scarcity.

This is a big one.

Scarcity creates an undercurrent of not enough-ness, of fear.

We are all moving closer to death. One of the many aims of yoga is to prepare us for death, to help us live in the now, so that we can truly experience life and stop any fear surrounding the end of our natural cycle. The ultimate surrender. For me, facing this earlier on in my life than I expected was so painful, but poignantly liberating.

Underlying yogic philosophy, is the idea, that we are all part of the whole, we come from the whole and will return to the whole. This, when embodied, helps us to see past the ego, and to return back to the light, bliss and stillness which is inside of us all, we just tend to forget about it. We get distracted. Our egos are amazing, they are so needed, they drive us, motivate us, inspire us and enable us to have a sense of self, that we need to live as an individual on this earth. However, quite often they can tend to dominate and overshadow our light, our souls. The ego is often responsible for pulling us away from our centre.

There is so much rushing in our world, it is so woven into our language, it gives us an insidious false sense of scarcity, that takes us away from peace and revs up our already over stimulated nervous systems. Language, like, 'quick get this', 'limited offer', 'don't miss out,' creating FOMO and anxiety to buy and do. The media and the news thrives on fear, scarcity, not enough-ness, power struggles and polarity.

By the nature of being human and having an ego, we will all have an underlying fear of death, that we might not be aware of. This grasping of life creates an energy of fear that vibrates, unseen, throughout our body, unless we learn to see it, stop turning away from it, stop pretending it doesn't exist, shine a light on it and accept it.

If we haven't surrendered to it, we tend to fight it, we try and cram as much into 'the time that we have' as possible. An attempt in our minds to fight against the natural order, to make the most of our time. Reflected in the belief that we only have one life, that we have got to make it count.

'Making it count,' what does that mean? Everyone has different views about how life should be lived.

Can't living as you, just living your life, as the beautiful unique soul that you are, be enough?

Surely that is it?

I hope, that we don't have to justify our existence on this planet by how many hours we stay active, or by justifying what we have spent our time doing.

Was it value packed enough?

Who decides?

You do.

You are far more than enough, you are perfect and you do not need to prove anything to anyone.

Live your life on your terms.

Use your time doing the things that light you up.

Use self awareness to discover what you love doing, how much space you need, how much down time you need in your life.

You create your reality.

The reality you create reflects the love that you have for yourself.

Start to love yourself more, to really care for yourself.

I see my life as a practise, one moment at a time, one step at a time. I practise being mindful. I practise quietening fear. I say practise, because this is exactly what it is. I will always fall back into fear and judging myself at different points in my life. I just will. I accept that. Each time I will remind myself of my beautiful humanness. I don't believe that I will be enlightened on this earth walk. I love being human. I love that my soul chose this body, with the people in my life, with both the challenges and the joy, the wild and the normal experiences, for the growth of my soul. This is my belief. So I practise aligned with this.

Sometimes I manage it, sometimes I don't.

Does the concept of time loom over me still? Sometimes. Not very often now, but when it does, it is like a force, making me rush, hurry the things that shouldn't be hurried, miss moments when I should have felt peaceful. I just notice it now though, with a lot more ease than I used to.

I accept that I will die.

I accept that I live in a world that measures success differently to me, and I let that all go.

I don't want my life to feel like a rush. I want my life to feel delicious.

I made a promise to myself to live. To do all that I can to find the life in each breath, to let joy infuse my breath.

I made a promise to not allow the breath that accompanies panic, scarcity, rushing and pressure to fill the majority of my life.

I choose to breathe deeply.

I choose to live deeply.

These are daily, conscious choices that I make.

As I write this, I feel my breath slow down. I feel the tears fill my eyes. Another gentle sweet healing. Another part of me that still believed in rushing, has softened and let go.

I am grateful.

We have been well and truly programmed. We have been trained to follow a linear, human created, construct of time. Society as a whole has complied. We have fully embodied this linear concept of time and structured our lives according to it.

I am so tired of the hold that time has had over me and appears to have over us, in modern societies. Our programming began at school, and it carries on enticing us away from our true nature, from the natural workings of our body. Our bodies are so wise, they have their own body clocks, the circadian rhythms, they know what they need to function, when to get up and when to rest. Yet we get trained to ignore this inner knowing. To strive for the worth that is given to us for being busy or working for longer hours than is good for our minds, bodies and souls. All the worth attached to measurements, all false, all artificial constructs.

Teenagers physiologically are designed to wake up later in the morning and are at their best in the afternoon, yet we force them to get up to the schedule of others, to fit in with the linear, to not maximise their natural energetic rhythm. It's easier for the systems we have in place, way more convenient.

Adults as a norm are required to fit into the 9-5, five days a week, it's more efficient for capitalism. Some of us are natural early birds, it is programmed into our DNA. The early birds would get up early and start gathering supplies for the tribe. Some of us are night owls, who would have kept watch at night and tended the fires. Some of us so desperately need naps, some of us don't. We are all unique, we all have our own internal rhythm, is this ever honoured? Is it ever mentioned in school? Are we taught to listen to our bodies ever in mainstream society?

As humans, we are so beautifully connected to each other, and at the same time, we are also our own unique piece, in a global and universal jigsaw puzzle. But it feels as though society wants us to all blend in, to all morph into a man made system and mental constructs.

I am still in the process of reconditioning myself after years of being an entrepreneur, answering only to the schedule that I have created. I call myself a recovering workaholic, as I still feel the pressure to rush and be as productive as I can. I have been programmed well.

My soul craves to stay more connected to nature, to rise when the sun comes up, to go within, and start to wind down for bed when the sun starts its descent. Our bodies have inner codes and complex systems to trigger us to wake up as the sky lightens. As the temperature of the evening starts to drop, becoming cooler than the day, our bodies take these cues, and respond by preparing for sleep. This is the role of our circadian rhythms, which is inextricably linked to the external natural world that we inhabit, and gets disrupted by caffeine, artificial light and the structures that we abide by in our societies.

To listen and to live aligned to our bodies innate inner wisdom, we would in effect need to 'rebel'. It feels to me, that if we all honoured our own body clocks and live aligned to our own unique inner rhythms, (which would lead us to be more vital, rested and overall healthier), we would have to move away from the structures that society has in place. We wouldn't be able to 'fit' our lives into the current system, this feels so restrictive to my soul. It sounds like we are living in a box doesn't it? To know that we are all conforming to a way of being, a way that has been dictated to us as 'the way,' that could actually be damaging to our mental and physical wellness.

Is there another way? A way that honours our bodies natural way of finding homeostasis? Of course, there will be, but as humans we love the known. The unknown is scary and feels out of control, so we have the tendency to remain in the status quo. I hope over time, more possibility for flexibility will open up.

Nature works in cycles and we are part of nature, we are not separate. We are designed to operate in synchronicity with the world around us. Nature doesn't just keep going on a linear path, or keep doing, or being productive. Nature knows that in order to fire on all cylinders in spring and summer, she needs some proper restorative deep rest. She needs to be quiet, to be in the dark to find inspiration so that she can be ignited for growth again. She needs to let go of what is no longer serving her, to conserve her energy. For mother earth, autumn is a time of letting go, and winter of resting. This is the natural balance of yin and yang, rest, action, dark, light, we need it all, sometimes more yin as in autumn and winter. Sometimes more yang. Yet we are in a society that honours the yang, and for the main part ignores the need for rest. Sometimes rest can even be shamed, and labelled as being lazy.

No.

Rest is your birthright and is necessary for your wellness and vitality. Deep restorative rest and sleep is so needed for our emotional and physical wellbeing. Sleep and rest are not luxuries, they are necessities, and should be prioritised. If anything, the number of hours that we sleep should be a number that is praised and celebrated more than the hours that we have worked.

You need it all, the rest and the action. Nature and humans need balance, the body is always trying to move towards homeostasis. This can be achieved by honouring your body, listening to it, and living in a more cyclical way.

The book that helped me to rewrite and redefine my relationship to time is the 'Big Leap' by Gay Hendricks (7). It is such a long time ago that I read it, so I won't quote from it. But, I highly recommend that you have a read, it is an amazing book with so many lessons in it. It also helps you see where you set limits, in the form of neuro-set points in your own mind. These points define how much joy and growth you allow yourself to experience. If you have never investigated this before, it is well worth reading as a starting point.

As an aside, I love the fact that we will all read the same books and all come away with different learnings, different views, and different interpretations of what we read. Most likely our experience and take aways from reading a book, may be wildly different from the intention of the author. This is why I love listening to what others think, we all see things so differently, we are designed too. I know that I would love to hear your interpretation of that book, you would see something that I didn't see, and your interpretation of it would change the way that I see things. We all have so much to learn from each other if we stay open, stay curious, and really listen with an open heart.

Before I read that book, I thought that I was busier and had less time that I actually did. I was stuck in the linear concept of time and scarcity, and gave my power away to it, rather than take ownership of how I was spending my 3D time allowance. As a remedy, to soothe my wired nervous system, I stopped and looked at the language I was using to talk about time.

I stopped saying the phrases listed below, that I had encoded in my way of being on autopilot as responses.

"No, sorry, I can't, I don't have time"

"I won't ask them, I know they don't have time."

"I need more hours in the day."

"I'm running out of time."

"I never have enough time."

"Quick, the clock is ticking."

Can you hear the lack, the sense of panic, the disempowerment, the urgency in all of those sayings? The scarcity, the fear, the victim mentality? This was all constantly running around my head, shaping the way that I experienced life.

Here is an invitation for you. To take an intentional pause and read through the limiting thoughts that I have listed above, that used to belong to me. As you read through them, ask yourself, how does it feel for you? Do I seem empowered or like a victim? Do any give you a physical response in your body? Any revelations or a-ha's?

To free myself of this underlying feeling of scarcity, that was in effect pervading all of my life and nervous system, I decided to take them one at a time and reframe them to take my power back. I took great care and delight in crafting different responses to common scenarios in my life, using words and sentences that didn't give my sovereignty away. I practised them. I said them out loud to myself, over and over again. Then I played with them. Over time, I embodied them. I caught myself when I was responding to people in the old way, and chose to use my new phrases. It felt so strange and uncomfortable at first, but after I settled into this new way of being, it felt so liberating.

Here is my process of reframing. I started with what I wanted to stop saying.

"No, sorry, I can't, I don't have time."

This is something that I said automatically if I didn't want to do something. I became aware of it. I ignored the little inward wince that I did as I observed myself saying it. I was in effect lying. When I said these automatic sentences.

I was avoiding the conversations and the truth about how I choose to allocate my time. I wasn't honouring my own agency or being truthful with others. Honesty and authenticity are some of my top values, it is important for me to live in alignment with them.

I will tell you a little story. I have a friend whom I love dearly, and absolutely love spending time with. A few years ago (pre pandemic) I was working a lot of nights and weekends at my yoga studio. The free weekends that I had were precious time with my family. My friend asked if I wanted to go for a walk at the weekend. The pre a-ha me, would have said, "No, sorry, I can't, I don't have time." This wasn't true and I had promised myself that I would stop saying it. How was I going to get back to her and articulate to her in a different way? I found the answer. THE TRUTH. I decided to be honest.

My response was, "I always love seeing you, I can't wait to see you, I miss you, but I have been working so many weekends and nights at the moment for my business, I am dedicating my weekends to family time. Have you still got space in the week to meet up? If so what days and times are good for you?" We met up in the week, and shared the most beautiful walk together.

Sometimes, I might just say, "No thank you," or "I don't enjoy doing that, could we do something else?" This means that I don't spend my energy, doing things that I don't like.

You feel it when someone is with you and doing something that they don't like just because they think it will make you happy. It doesn't feel good energetically on either side. I would much rather someone say to me, "No, I don't like that, but I do love doing this, if you would like to." If we both do, what a beautiful and deeper way of spending time together. Free from irritations and resentment, which comes along with you, when you are doing something that you don't want to. Try as hard as you like, that energy comes with you.

I totally recognise that it might feel really awkward to start to express yourself in this way. We are after all programmed to people please. Honesty and open hearted conversations, might be uncomfortable for a few minutes, but with practise they get easier. A life with more joy, starts to be possible. When we up-level our energetic wellness, we show the way for others to start to look after their own energy more, and decondition from people pleasing.

This next old saying of mine, was a big one for me.

"I won't ask them, I know they don't have time."

This was all around my lack of self worth. I think because I used to people please and spend a lot of time doing things that I didn't want to do. I didn't want anyone else to ever feel that way doing something that I had asked them to do. I didn't want anyone to people please on my behalf. So I put barriers up in order to protect them.

On reflection, I can see how crazy this is. In effect, I am telling myself that I know everything about that other soul. I know what they are thinking, pre-empting that they won't want to do that thing with me. Both sides could well have missed out on so many amazing opportunities. I also got into the habit of doing a lot of things by myself because of this limiting belief.

I hold so much compassion for that version of me.

I just didn't feel enough.

I thought that I wasn't enough for other people, that I would be forcing them to spend time with me and they wouldn't want to. That it would be awkward for them to say "No." I had a problem with boundaries. It all stemmed from my perception and not enough-ness being projected outwards to the world around me and everyone in it.

When this thought pops into my head, I say to myself, "I will just invite them, I know that they have their own sovereignty, that they are in control of their own lives and that they are free to say no. It is not my place to make their decisions for them."

This really is what my head is like. I observe my thoughts. I am in the constant process of getting over myself and my ego, one thought at a time. Believe me, my ego loves deciding what everyone else thinks and presuming to know what they want to do. But it's not my job, and I am slowly but surely releasing control.

Instead of "I need more hours in the day." I choose other words to tell myself.

"I have an abundance of time." Or "I decide what I do in my day."

Instead of "I'm running out of time." I say, "I have an abundance of time." "I decide how time feels for me." or "I choose to work in the quantum time, there is no lack there."

Instead of "I never have enough time." I say, "I have all the time that I need." Or, "If I don't get done all that I planned to do today, it can wait, or I can ask for help. It is all okay."

Instead of "Quick, the clock is ticking." I say, "My concept of time determines how time feels to me, I will slow down and be present in this moment."

Can you sense the calm running through your nervous system as you read and feel into the reframed sentences? Can you feel the shift into empowerment and sovereignty?

As you choose your responses and move away from the selection of autopilot phrases that you have learnt from others, you move away from any victim mentality around time, you reclaim your power.

Time is a measurement. Your experience of life, is so much more than that.

I can't remember who said this beautiful phrase, or the exact words, but for me, it really encapsulates the magic of reclaiming your relationship to time.

"If you are not present, you are choosing to walk away from the present moment."

Let's look at the programs in your beautiful mind, which might take some time (ironically).

Take another pause, be with this section of the book. Go deep. It will change your experience of life. As always, awareness first, observation of the weird and wonderful thoughts that run around your mind, and then, start to work your own magic in healing. Begin to transition into to a place of sovereignty with your experience of time by reframing your language.

When I began this journey towards my own freedom, this is the path that I followed. For me it felt like freedom, as my beliefs were keeping me small, keeping me in a mindset and energetic frequency of lack, scarcity, not enough-ness, and generally feeling powerless. It all started to unravel here, and I am so excited for you.

Let's take a dive into your mind. An invitation to contemplate these questions, with love, objectivity and compassion.

What programs around time do you think or feel that your brain has downloaded and installed from others and society?

What programs are running constantly in the background? Which are yours and which aren't?

What do these thoughts cause you to believe right now?

What words does this belief cause you to use right now?

Is any of it yours?

Is any of it true?

Now some deeper inquiry.

How do you use your time? Take a few days in the week and audit it. You can print out a calendar that has 10/15 minute sections have it with you and record everything, tea break (or lack of), scrolling (yes!), Netflix, exercise, cuddling your children, work, everything … This is the start of awareness.

How do these days feel? Spacious, rushed, hurried? Is this how you want to feel? We will look more at this is the busy section, just note, just let the awareness start to cultivate.

Notice again, without judgement, the phrases and words that you say to yourself and others about time. Observe and note them.

What are other people around you saying or have said about time, go back to school, parents, grandparents, friends, write it all down.

What are your beliefs around time?

Do you give your sovereignty away to it?

Divide a piece of paper into two with a line, look at your list of all the above, write them down on one side, highlight the ones that are true, leave the ones that aren't true. The mind might trick you into believing that they are all true, sit with them, slow your breath, place your hand on your heart, ask your soul, ask your body, not your mind, is it really true? Go beneath the programming.

Connect in with the you before you got programmed.

The you, before you gave your power away.

With the list, anything that is highlighted, double check, is it true? If it is, can you reframe slightly, is there anything you can make more graceful, more you? With the beliefs and phrases that aren't true, what can you say as an alternative? Write them down in the second column, speak them out loud, see how they feel.

Now practise, be playful, be curious. Approach it as an experiment.

You are choosing a new way of being, it is natural for it to feel strange and uncomfortable at the beginning.

Take baby steps.

Laugh when you slip into your old ways.

Remember that you are beautifully human, you are perfectly you, and you are way more than enough.

Sprinkle it all, with self compassion, humour and tenderness.

Slow down sweet soul
Place your feet on the ground
Put your hands on your heart
Breathe in …
Breathe out …

Slow down sweet soul

Why so fast?
Why the rapid heartbeat?
Why so concerned?
Why so bothered about the concept of time?
It's man made you know
The ancient greeks, they knew
That time was not linear
They knew that it is never ending
A circle, like the womb
A void, pure limitless potential
All there for you sweet soul

You are limitless
You are timeless

Slow down sweet soul
Stop turning outside
Turn inside
Thats where you are
Thats where your heart resides
Your Soul will go on forever
So what legacy are you here to leave?
She rushed around all the time
She was always on time
She was so good at moaning

Or do you want to leave a legacy of serenity
Of calm
Of grace
Do you want everyone to remember how they felt around you
How your energy enveloped them
With love, with heart, with peace
The thing is sweet soul its your choice
I will ask you again
Why so fast?
Always rushing around to the beat of other peoples dreams
Other peoples expectations

What about you sweet soul?
Remember you
You matter
I see you
Take the time to see you too

CHAPTER SEVEN
WHEN DID BUSY BECOME A BADGE OF HONOUR?

This chapter might be interesting for you, especially if you have attached (like I did) your worth to being busy.

As a teacher, coach, mentor, and writer, I can only share from my lens of perception. That view has been shaped by my experience of life, and by my own operating programs. Only I could write this book in this way, only you will read and interpret this book in your own unique way.

I believe in synchronicity. I believe that you have this book in your hand for a reason. To look at life, patterns and behaviour through my lens of perception for the time that you spend with these pages. Not to take it all on, or to believe everything that I say. That will never be my aim. I wish that by seeing the way that I view life, seeing through my eyes for a short while, will inspire you, maybe irritate and trigger you. Some things might cause you to not like me very much, you might feel a little angry. Whenever this happens with my client's and students, I always say, "perfect." This is what I am here for, to be a mirror. To help you see where the parts of your essence and your light are being suppressed. To help you start to inquire where your beliefs, values and desire for your life's expression are, and identify where others may have encroached into your beautiful energetic field and temporarily tapped into your power.

This inquiry, these realisations that you will have, may be uncomfortable at times.

If you have been drawn to this book to heal and start your transformation, you will be triggered. Embrace it, shout it out to yourself or the world. "YES! I have found something to let go of. I have found a thread to pull to unbind me from the beliefs and the limits that are holding me back. I am ready to step back into my power. I am ready to make my way out of the status quo, out of stagnation and grow. I am ready."

You might have been drawn to this book, to read it in order to be able to let others know about it. Sometimes the teachings and healing that another would benefit from, are best received from an impartial source.

This chapter was inspired by a moment I remember so vividly, a moment that actually shook me energetically. I hadn't seen a friend for a while, when we finally met, I asked him how he was and his reply word for word was, "Yeah, good, busy, busy." I looked at him and didn't praise him for it. I asked him, "How is that? Are you okay with that?" He looked stunned, no answer, and the conversation abruptly pivoted onto something else. The thing is though, I didn't ask him how busy he was, I asked him how he was. I wanted to know how his heart was, had he been having fun, was he sad? It was one of those moments when I could see things so clearly, a pattern of disconnection in our world. A disconnection from self and each other.

Following this moment, I started to notice it everywhere. It felt like the word 'busy' was being used like the word 'overwhelm' and the phrase, "I don't have time." Like an umbrella or a blanket to hide behind, so we don't have to reveal the truth to ourselves and others. So we don't have to have the deep conversations, or face our own discomfort.

In the moment that I mention above, it was as though time had come to a standstill, and the world was swirling around me. I felt such deep sadness. Through our use of socially acceptable words and phrases, it feels to me like we have lost so much depth. We have turned our conversations into superficial experiences.

I love to feel the person I am talking to energetically, to see them, to see the soul beneath the facade that we all wear to some extent to be accepted.

Where are you?

With my friend, I craved a deeper connection.

I don't believe that every conversation should be deep, light is fun, it is so needed, there is a right timing and a right place for every exchange. But maybe lots more of us, would benefit from a heart to heart exchange more often?

The word 'busy' implies value again. A sense of being measured by the facts and figures that society loves so much. Busy equates to lots of activity, hints at productivity, and our supposed worth. It doesn't feel like it values rest, only the possibility of earning potential, using your energy, lots of doing, must not sit still, must keep going. I want to look at the no rest aspect. The all pervading guilt that I have had to decondition myself from.

When I was a stay at home mum, for 6 months before I started studying again, my husband had never ever said to me, that I shouldn't sit down, that I shouldn't rest, that every second of my day I should be working. I would never dream of expecting this from anyone else. I want people to rest when they are tired, to slow down, to honour their body, and emotions. Yet in the distant past, I didn't hold that true for myself. I could have been on the go all day and just sat down, if my husband walked in the door at that moment, I would get up and look busy. What on earth was that really all about? It was all self driven, by my internal programs.

So I started to look, and it went deep. It is trained behaviour, instilled in us to be good workers. Through our society, we are taught, that we have to work hard, rest is for the weak. We hear sayings such as, "I will rest when I'm dead," this phraseology is insidious, it infiltrates our energetic system. On a sub-conscious level it has such a massive impact on how we live, if we take those beliefs on as our own.

The work, the hustle mentality, all the language, the phrases we have to keep us working hard, compliant for the well-oiled machine that is capitalism. The belief that we work hard and then we will be free to do all the things that light us up, that we really love, when we retire.

I have a story with the phrase, "I'll do that when I retire." For my 47th birthday, I had a strong urge to paint. I loved painting when I was at school, I have sketched a bit since, but not painted. I caught the thought in my head. "I will take some art classes when I am retired." I got a full body shock. What was I thinking? I was setting a limit upon not allocating any time to doing something that I really wanted to do. So I asked for paint for my birthday and off I went. Pure joy. Abstract art flowed out of me and I sold two pieces. Painting is now a part of my life and creative expression. I could have stopped all of that with a line of programmed code.

When did we forget that we are humans? That we are not robots, that our bodies need downtime for recalibration and healing. That our nervous systems need time to stop and rest. That we don't do well with constant notifications alerting our stress system all the time. Nowadays, unless we notice it, we are on all the time, unless we choose to consciously unplug.

To do that, we have to be aware, and feel enough, care about ourselves enough, love ourselves enough, to choose and then take a different course of action.

After my first breast cancer episode, I got into busy mode. I got busy fundraising, jumping out of planes, filling every moment with busyness, attempting the three peaks challenge. I started running, go go go, let's live, let's fill every moment, let's make this life count. All triggered by scarcity and not feeling enough.

What I realised the second time around, is that I was in my beautiful humanness, frantically avoiding the eventuality of my own death. I wasn't thinking that living life as me, in the small moments, was enough. I was believing that life should be full of one big and dramatic moment after another. I was avoiding the beauty that is in each moment, the beauty in the small details that make up life. I was swinging from one thing to the next. I was exhausted in so many ways. I was avoiding the feeling of all the trauma that I had acquired from the experience of having cancer.

I was repressing it.

It came up for me to heal in the form of general anxiety, which I managed to nip in the bud early. Now my wellness, my living in the moment, is my life, and my priority.

Instead of aiming to be busy, my goals now are to have a more spacious, present life.

To do this, I ask myself.

How am I feeling?

Am I rested?

Do I have space around events?

Am I having heart connections and conversations?

The other night a group of friends were supposed to meet up, it went wrong and we didn't. But for a while there were messages back and forth saying things like, "well I could meet for 30 minutes." My friends were trying to 'fit it all in'. I just said "No thank you, let's reschedule." I want to be with my friends fully, to relax, to be present, to have Kairos time, the quantum, blissful, recharging time. Not the Chronos squeezed and compressed version of time. Not a rushed glimpse of them where they are only partially with me and half of their being is in the next moment, waiting and ready to go.

I crave slow luxurious time, deep chats, not a collection of rushed moments.

With my inquiry, I naturally began to change. I learnt that for me, life isn't the events that I cram into my hours. It is the experience, the feelings that I have within the construct of these man made hours.

Life is lived in the moment. Busy is counterintuitive to that. Busy leads to burnout. People come to me for yoga, healing, life, business and spiritual mentorship. They come needing more space, their souls are craving it. Craving more grace, ease and desperately needing to move away from exhaustion.

It sometimes feels like society has come to view burnout as something that happens naturally. It has an air of normality around it, of social acceptance.

My heart wants to scream "No." We, as humans have created the conditions for this. Behind every case of burnout is a human being, a body, a mind, a soul, an energetic system, that has been pushed to their limits and beyond.

This should never be any kind of normal.

I have learnt that being busy, keeping doing, instead of being, can be a trauma response. It makes so much sense to me now. I have so much love and compassion for that version of myself that I look back on. Just trying to keep her head above her feelings, above the many different flavours of 'whelm,' that she was so desperately trying to run away from.

I invite you to take a pause. I hope that you are getting used to these now and honouring yourself in this way. Open your journal, make a drink, and ask yourself these questions, with honesty and compassion.

In everyday life, are you keeping busy, are you always doing?

Are you managing to stay present?

Are you relaxed?

How is your nervous system?

Are you getting enough space, the space that you really need, not the space that your mind deems is just enough?

Are you feeling tired a lot, or worried about hitting burnout?

Is there a nagging deep down in your soul that you are avoiding something by constantly doing?

We can also get stuck in the things that we think we have to do. As I share some of the language and phrases I used to use or be influenced by, have an audit to see whether they are part of your vocabulary.

"You've made your bed, now lie in it."

This statement to me, feels like a straitjacket. Especially for a multi faceted, multi-passionate being. In effect this phrase is telling us that when we make a big decision in our life, that's it now, thats what you chose to do. How on earth could this ever be? You are allowed to change your mind, to respond to life, to grow, to expand.

One of my teachers Sahara Rose(8) compares living your dharma (spiritual life purpose) to a mountain range. You get up one mountain, you are so focused upon that, you don't see all the other beautiful mountain peaks and possibilities until you get to the top. Once you get there, life opens up. You are different. Climbing that mountain, the experiences you had along the way, your inner dialogue and the encounters you had with others, will all cause you to change, to be a different version of the you that started out on your journey. Your soul is here to evolve, at different stages in your life, you will need different things. Especially if you are choosing to grow and not stay stagnant. But, if you choose being busy, doing the things that you are already doing, where is the space for growth and expansion? Are there any pauses, places or opportunities for you to pivot and adjust on your path? I love this subject so much, this is what I have chosen to coach souls in, and I dedicate my own life to being multi-passionate and multi-dimensional without limits.

I am so blessed that I have always allowed myself the space and grace to pivot. It has meant in the past, before I fully owned my sovereignty, that I had to wear the warrior woman shield of protection to repel the comments that were directed at me. Questioning, why I am doing something different, being told how faddy I am. When I look back at my journey, I have always been perfectly on track, learning the things I needed to learn, feeling what I needed to feel and also experiencing what I don't want to feel. The freedom with which I allowed myself to live has enabled me to have the wild and wonderful experiences that have led me here, to this wealth of holistic, spiritual and cultural knowledge. And more importantly, a lifetime of embodied practise that enables me to hold beautiful space for my clients and students. To share my wisdom, and to keep my connection to the universe open. I own all of this. Now I live this way of being without having to be the warrior woman, that I once felt was so important to be.

Just because something has been the same for a long time, or something has always been done a certain way, do we need to keep doing the same things? As humans with brains that like to be comfortable, we tend to hang out in the status quo, to lean towards keeping the same things going. Since I identified that growth and freedom are amongst my top values, I question everything. If I don't, I know that I have the tendency to stay in fear and stagnation.

I invite you to get into the habit of asking yourself regularly, if what you are doing, what you are spending your precious energy and resources on is necessary? Or is it just busyness?

I love this story that really stuck with me, and illustrates the freedom you can get from questioning, and trying something different. In the book 'Essentialism: The

Disciplined Pursuit of Less' - Greg McKeown,(9) tells the story of a man in an office environment. He had to do the same report every week. One day, he decided just not to do it. No one ever noticed. One less thing to give his time and busyness away to.

We all have some of these things in our work and private life, things that might have been useful, perhaps even essential once. As we are always changing, and everything and everyone around us are always changing, the things that we once did, that once mattered, can become redundant, or might need to be done differently. In my business, I always have intentional pauses and audits, in the house too. How are things operating? What has changed? What can I let go of? What can I simplify? I am always seeking growth, and simplification, more ease, never the status quo.

We can also get busy as a means of 'people pleasing,' because we just don't want to say "No." Because we don't know our own boundaries, and if we do, we don't want to express them to others, we are scared of conflict, of speaking our truth, of being seen, of stating our desires.

We say "yes" to things, that our heart longs to say "no" to. The questions that you asked yourself in the 'Time' section are perfect to do for 'Busy'. The two are so closely woven together.

As humans, we also like to hide, behind being busy. A typical response to the question, "Would you like to go and see that show next week?" Is often, "Sorry, I can't I am so busy."

If you wanted to see that person but not the show, would it be better to hear, "I don't like shows, they aren't my thing, but I would love to do something else with you." Honesty connects us, so deeply.

Hiding behind a mask, is exhausting. Not living aligned with your truth is exhausting. Doing what you think people expect of you is exhausting.

That isn't a feeling that I want to actively keep feeling in this beautiful life of mine.

What about you?

Let's flip the perspective. If we ask a friend to do something with us, and they are exhausted, but they feel that they 'should' come out. Would you rather that they opt to stay at home and nourish themselves and recharge, so that they can spend time with you when they are feeling more energetic, when they can be present and want to be there?

I want experiences dialled up to the maximum. I don't want energetic exchanges with people who are half there, half with me, half longing to be in bed or somewhere else. That energy can be felt. I want experiences on the highest frequency, in full expression.

When my kids or husband interrupt me when I am in the middle of something, I ask them to give me a minute so that I can finish what I am doing, then I tell them, "I am all yours." I put the phone down or close the laptop, face them and am fully with them. My attention is with them, not half on what I was doing.

I stop the doing, to be present.

As mentioned earlier, with my self observation, I noticed that I had slipped into a habit of doing everything on my list, which was always long, (an overachiever in recovery here) and then started adding the next days tasks to it. It grew and grew and was never ending. It was impossible for me to finish my list. I still fall into this way of being occasionally.

What was I doing to myself? I was stuck in the old paradigm. I must keep busy, got to keep going.

I wasn't allowing myself the bonus of being able to work efficiently and quickly, to get everything that I needed done and then rest, or do something for fun, something creative, to nourish my soul. That makes me sad to remember, as that shows how little I thought of myself. How little I honoured myself.

I made myself keep on keeping on. I was the harshest most critical taskmaster for myself.

Now, I schedule way less in and make space for blissful nothingness. In the spiritual world that I inhabit, it is in the nothing that everything is. I let my mind wander, I contemplate, I read, I doodle, I paint, I have daily cacao ceremonies, I anoint my body with pure essential oils, I journal, create a card spread, have daily movement. I nurture myself. That might sound busy to you, but it is my spiritual nourishment. It slows me down, it grounds me, it is my priority. I have a daily practise that my soul craves to be done before I do my 'outward facing work' or even 'parenting'.

If my mind gets tired, or if my creativity stops flowing, if I start to notice feelings of frustration or any resentment for any aspect of my work, or get even a hint of feeling busy. I stop now. Literally in that moment of awareness, I stop. I down tools. In its place, I move, meditate, cook, read, and give myself the permission to take some time off. Often, the moment, I have made that space, and taken the pressure off, the moment I free myself from the feeling of busy, the creativity starts to flow again. I get enthused and can't help but get back to what I was doing, re-energised. We are so good at blocking our own energy, with this forceful way of living, keeping on powering through. This is the hustle culture. This is the old paradigm.

'Busy' takes my power away, and aligned action, moves me towards freedom and expansion. I know that I will occasionally get stuck into the groove of being busy, (beautiful humanness), but I catch myself, and have vowed to keep being there for myself and catching myself time and time again.

In order to stop giving my power away to the concept of being 'busy,' I had to start to look at my priorities, to assess what was truly important to me.

The thing about prioritising, is that you have to get honest with yourself as to what truly matters to you. This can be challenging, especially if you have never thought about it before. I can remember the first time I began to to inquire, I cried. I didn't even know what I wanted to do, what gave me joy anymore outside of my family, let alone what I wanted to prioritise. I had fallen completely out of touch with myself. I was pretty numb.

When you do discover what you want to do, this then means change, conversations with loved ones, rocking the boat, tipping the old apple cart. It takes strength, it takes sovereignty, it takes owning you're worth. It's one step at a time towards throwing busy away and moving towards the things that bring you joy.

I am going to invite you to look at the points of inquiry below that I hope will bring you so much light, joy and love.

Reflect from the audit work that you did with time. Is there any general busy-ness, or things that feel busy? Make a list. Can you let go of anything, or delegate like the man in the Essentialism book?

Do you have space to just be?

Are you doing things for the sake of it?

Notice what others around you say, or have said in the past about being busy. Reflect back to school days, parents, grandparents, friends, write it all down.

What are your beliefs around being busy? Do you give your sovereignty away to it?

With the beliefs and phrases that aren't true, what can

you say as an alternative? Write them down, speak them out loud, see how they feel.

One of my favourite things to ask my client's to do, is to make a joy list. Write down all the things that you love to do, or have been craving to do. Choose one, be brave tell others that your soul longs to do this, and make it happen. Start to live the life that you desire.

You are allowed to want and desire things for yourself. Joy is your birthright. A reminder that you are light, what you do matters and you matter.

The Space around

You can see more clearly
In more definition
When there is space around

Too jammed in
Too cluttered
No space to breathe

Everything merges
Intertwined
When there is no space around

I can't see or feel
Where I begin
Where you end

No space between

CHAPTER EIGHT
THE REASONS NOT TO I CAN'T, I SHOULD, I MUST, I NEED

This list could go on forever, with phrases that we all use, creating beliefs that attempt to limit our fabulousness and potential. I am guessing that you have a long list of reasons like I did, as to why you shouldn't do something. And maybe an even longer list of reasons as to why you aren't good enough.

My goodness, my list was long. I had a seemingly infinite list of excuses, words, phrases and deep seated beliefs that I gave my power away to.

I affectionately call them '*the reasons not to*'.

As we notice them, and start to shine the light of awareness onto them, we can bring them out of the shadows into the mind and into the light. We can take it further for more transformation and get them onto paper. This transference from my own experience, onto paper, or spoken out loud, is powerful. It gets them all out of my head, so they aren't just circulating unknown to myself, or carrying on running my internal programs. By doing this, I can also see them for what they are, lies, untruths, energetic and mental binds.

Although most of them are often untruths, there are some of my '*reasons not to*' that are valid. I will share the processes that have been so helpful for me, when looking at these pesky '*reasons not to*'.

It was during a teaching from a beautiful coach, and amazing being, Deb Erickson, the founder of the I Can Institute, that I received a profound a-ha moment. You know the ones, when you might have heard the same message over and over, but it doesn't quite align in your being? It was one of those, a moment that changed everything for me. (10)

She simply said, that when we say, "I can't" we are choosing 'Not to'.

That was it, life changed, with such a simple sentence.

The realisation, that I always have a choice.

Everything I do, is my personal choice. Everything in my life at present and in the past, is a literal manifestation of the choices that I made and continue to make.

Have a little pause. Let that be with you for a moment, how does it feel?

When you say, "I can't" you are choosing 'not to'.

Did you already know and live this fully? Or is part of your ego, any aspect of the facade that you are hiding behind screaming at the words? Does part of you still think, I can't choose? Did you involuntarily shake your head, screw your face up, put the book down? Or wanted to?

Observe.

No judgement, just notice.

This is illuminating your beliefs. Bringing them out into the light, gently prodding them with awareness. I know this, because I still regularly scream and shake my head at a book that has said something that I know will cause me to grow. That my ego doesn't want to look at, because my mind knows that it will involve change. In that moment, I might be quite happy with the status quo, comfortable and safe.

When I have been triggered, when my next potential opportunity for growth has been illuminated, I have trained myself to listen to my body and my soul. My being always whispers to me. Now, after a lifetime of ignoring it, I am able to listen to it, to create the space and stillness to hear it. Deep down, in my soul, I am lit up at the thought of casting off another limiting belief, of freeing myself a little bit more, healing another layer and stepping into a deeper level of my expression.

Practises that quiet your mind, are so powerful in aiding this. Meditation, running, pranayama, yoga, knitting. Whatever it is for you, make the opportunity to have space in your mind. Prioritise the rituals that quiet your mind and bring you back into your body, so that you can hear and feel the wisdom deep within you. So that you can connect with the innate inner knowing that you were born with, and have constant access to. This voice, this knowing, is often quieter than your ego, your mind and your thoughts. As you keep developing the listening skills, as you keep loving your ego, but asking it to settle, this is where growth is. Continue to observe how your body and inner knowing communicates with you. Start to recognise the sound of your inner voice.

The story of the second arrow, is a beautiful buddhist teaching which really resonated with me. It has been challenging to apply the lessons that it holds into my life in hard times. However, when I am able to embody the lesson, my suffering reduces. The teaching shows the power of choosing, over believing that you can't, thinking that you are powerless, or hanging in the energy of believing that you are a victim and that life is always happening to you.

I first heard this teaching from my dear yoga teacher, Andrea Kwiatkowski. (11) It was 3 years after my first cancer diagnosis and I was awaiting results from an MRI scan, following an initial CT scan. I was told that it appeared as though the initial cancer had spread to my liver. I was raw. I was terrified. I was not in a good head space. I was lying on my yoga mat, listening to my teacher impart this much needed life lesson.

She told the tale of the second arrow. Life with all its events, its twists and turns, by nature causes us to suffer. We inevitably encounter and endure physical and emotional pain over the course of our earth walk. This is the first arrow. Life, hardship, injuries, trauma, loss.

In this instance cancer was my first arrow. Andrea then went on to talk about the second arrow. Throughout our life, the second arrow, is in the bow, pointing at you, ready to be fired at any time, ready to cause even more suffering.

You get to choose whether this arrow is released from the bow, or not.

This teaching triggered me so much, as I realised that I was shooting the second arrow at myself and then thrashing around with my own thoughts, with the pain of the potential future, the pain of the unknown.

I have noted by being both a student and a teacher, that sometimes we take the teachings that the teacher includes into a class, as if they were chosen specifically for us. My ego used to wonder how my teachers knew to include that point that was so relevant for me. I have had students after class tell me that it felt like I had chosen that passage or teaching just for them. In these circumstances, I believe that the teachings are so emotive, or triggering, because the student is ready for the lesson and the healing that comes with it.

In yoga and buddhism, it is the mind and its attachments that cause suffering, our denial of the impermanence of life, resistance to it's ever changing nature. One of the aims of yoga is to still the mind with it's arrows, so that we can attain self-actualisation.

With this second arrow, I was choosing to suffer greatly. Every time I travelled into the imagined future, I was 'preparing for the worst,' 'not expecting the best,' so then I wouldn't be 'disappointed'. I was shooting the second arrow. Those arrows were causing anxiety, fear and deep sadness. Unbeknown to my conscious mind, I had hand picked and embedded some really unhelpful ways of seeing the world from the collective. I had taken them and woven them deeply into my own consciousness.

Just writing this, I have stopped and taken a pause to hold my hands over my heart and send love to that past version of myself. So lost. In so much pain.

I was preparing myself emotionally for having to leave our children, in my mind I believed that the more I played it out in my head, the easier it would be when the time came. I was mentally preparing to die, but not with ease or grace. It was with a reluctant ego, clinging on with all my might. This way of living and being was exhausting. The most devastating aspect of it all though, was that these mental gymnastics took me away from living and my inner peace.

When I finally got my results, 2 CT scans, 1 MRI scan and 1 radioactive P.E.T scan later, all was well. The cancer had not spread. All that emotion, in effect for nothing. Sure, it was all a possibility, but not guaranteed. My suffering was caused by my projection into the future, by my fear, that inhabited my mind.

The underlying philosophy of many of the worlds spiritual systems and especially the yogic and buddhist path, is that the mind, creates suffering. It forgets that we are one with the cosmic consciousness, it believes that we are just our body. The clinging on to the body, to the way it is, to the status quo causes the suffering. Everything changes, nothing can stay the same.

So, when I was diagnosed for real, a further 2 years later, I embodied and applied the teachings that I had gained during this initial test. By this time, I had lived with 5 years of constantly shooting myself with the second arrow. I was so tired and I was so sad.

In that period, I was terrified of the cancer returning. I was constantly checking my chest area. I had so much scar tissue in my upper body, from the radiotherapy and lumpectomy. It was impossible to be able to distinguish the surgery scars themselves, in order to identify any new lumps. It was like a nervous tick, feeling all the bumps, all the scars, both physical and emotional, time after time.

It was self torture.

I was choosing the second arrow.

As soon as I was told that the cancer was back, I chose to have a double mastectomy. I chose to feel free, and I chose to not give my power away anymore to my ego and its fear of leaving this world. I chose to live, like really, truly, deeply live.

I choose to take that second arrow out of the case, and to not shoot it ever again. The effort was just too much.

A few weeks before my double mastectomy, we went on a trip for a family celebration, with lots of friends and family. I became super present. I was with my loved ones and friends, in a beautiful location. I knew I would be out of action for 8 weeks, and any further into the future, I surrendered to. It was all in the unknown and I had learnt by then to stop going there. All I knew and was focusing upon was the fact that I was there in that moment. I wanted to enjoy my time, in that version of my body, in that moment.

No-one could believe how I could be there and enjoy myself, let alone have such a good carefree time. I chose to keep the second arrow in the bag. I chose to stop loading the arrow into the bow. I had a mantra, which I kept repeating, anytime my ego wanted to go into the future, or the 'what-if's'.

"I am here now, right in this moment. The operation is next week and I will deal with it then." That was it, over and over when my thoughts did creep in. The more I brought myself back to the present, the less intrusive the thoughts became, and I was able to have such an amazing time, filled with connection, joy, memories and so many laughs that still warm my heart now.

It was so liberating for me. In a traumatic time, I had settled my mind. I was able to enjoy life, to be in the present. I didn't bypass what was happening to me, I acknowledged it fully. I acknowledged that I was scared, and that the operation would be mentally and physically tough. But in those moments when I wasn't at hospital, when I wasn't on the operating table, or getting marked up, for today, in that moment, I was safe. I would leave all of those feelings to deal with on the actual day. When that was my present reality and not a perceived reality.

We have the power to soothe our nervous system with meditation, yoga, essential oils, the people we surround ourselves with, the things we focus on, the things we tell ourselves, the things we choose to think about and not think about. I feel that it is a beautiful time to remind you, that you have so much personal power.

You can have way more peace than you ever think is possible.

With the remembrance that your thoughts create your beliefs. Your beliefs inform your choices, which then create your experience of life. Life, in itself, your experience of it, your embodiment of it, what you do and how you are, how you interact with other people and the impact you have on the space that you inhabit on this earth walk is all for you to choose.

There is a pause at the end of this chapter for you to get curious, about all of your '*reasons not to*'. As they pop into your head write them down. Just reading this chapter may well start to illuminate the unseen, the thoughts, the programming that lurks in the background of your psyche, running the show, and directing your experiences. If you feel inspired now, grab the workbook, or your journal and let the energy flow.

Following my realisation of what Deb Erickson said, which felt like the best slap in my face that I could have ever received, I chose to literally not let myself believe in the sayings like, "I can't," "I should". "I must".

As a natural teacher and someone who just loves applying what I learn, transforming information and knowledge into wisdom. I got practical. I started to experiment with this new finding and over time created a deeply embodied way of being.

I chose to replace the "I can't" with "I choose".

"I choose" over and over again.

Say it with me.

"I choose."

"I choose."

"I choose."

I became my own re-programmer.

I get to choose.

You get to choose.

I was dedicated and devoted to myself. I wanted to be free of this old way that my mind had adopted.

You too, can become the director of your own experiences, when you take the consciousness back from your shadows and your programming.

Isn't this what we should be doing anyway? Be in conscious control of ourselves. Like a car without a mindful driver, damage, harm and sadness can be caused if the driver is careless and unaware. The body is the car and our awareness is the driver.

I chose to take control back, along with copious

amounts of surrendering to the universe.

The moment, I started to say to myself or anyone else "I can't" I stopped myself and just gently said to myself, "of course you can, what do you choose?"

Let me tell you a few stories, of what this actually looked like in my life, how I chose to embody this.

My thought: "I can't do the workout today. I am so busy and so tired."

My heart: "I really want to though, and it will take me closer towards my goals, I always feel better after."

In situations like this, where I have caught myself saying "I can't," I check in with my own energy. How am I feeling in my body? Am I tired? What have I been doing? Is it true? I could have been on a 10 mile hike and be ready for rest. What was my truth in that moment, or did my subconscious just give me a '*reason not to*?'

If I was tired, I started to speak to myself like I would to someone that I love. Okay, I am so genuinely tired, in fact, I am exhausted, so I will choose to rest today and meditate, or, it could even be, let's have a Netflix binge with no guilt and just really enjoy it. It always feels decadent to me when I tune out completely.

If I am not tired, and it was a '*reason not to,*' I choose to take this next step towards what I want to achieve. I know right now, it feels like I don't want to. I know I will feel so good and happy afterwards. I choose to honour my body. I

I choose to honour my goals. I choose to step into the temporary discomfort. I know that the hardest part will be to get my workout clothes on. That moment is when I choose, aligned, empowered action. It is when I choose to honour myself.

How does all that feel for you?

"I can't," "I should," all feel so disempowering for me now. I feel like I don't have a choice when I say those phrases. I feel like I give my power away.

The first option that I gave above, feels tender, and nurturing, it is me listening to my body, and leading myself. Sometimes we need to rest. Sometimes we need to move and sometimes the second option might be the most nourishing option. Learn to listen to yourself, make a conscious choice, be empowered, live your life, allow yourself to dream and to move towards your goals. You are wise. Your body is wise, it knows what you need. You just need to learn to listen to it, to let go of what you 'think' you should be doing.

I promised myself that when I hear "I can't" in my head, I will challenge myself and see what is really true for me in that moment. Now, when I hear myself say, "I can't" or '*another reason not to*' in my head, I groan inwardly, as I know that there will be some growth to follow, which often means discomfort and awkwardness.

I was teaching a yoga class at a time when I had my yoga studio. My students, in one class were mostly retired women. They were in tree pose, and my mind flashed back to when I taught children's yoga and I would get the kids to try and stay still whilst myself and others swirled around them like the wind, trying to take their attention off of the balance. Yep, I said it… "I can't do that". And yes, I chose to. My students held tree pose, whilst I ran around, making the sound of the wind, trying to put them off. We had such a laugh, we created a space of joy. I got over myself a little bit more, and all was well. Another fear softened, the fear of acting like a child in front of a group of grown up women, the fear of looking silly, these are the small steps towards liberation. One moment, one limit, one belief at a time, with you choosing. Your liberation, is your choice. It comes from you, not from others, not from outside of you.

I sincerely acknowledge that in life, there are real 3D limitations that do exist. These must be recognised, I am a dreamer and a realist too. We need the balance of both to have a grounded full bodied life.

This story shows how I apply some realism in my life when dealing with *'the reasons not to'*.

As part of my cancer treatment, I had radiotherapy which hardened the skin and muscles around the right side of my armpit and across my chest, and has caused intense tightness and physical restriction of movement. My muscles just aren't working as they did (at the moment, you never know, I am leaving the possibility of more healing open). I have also had some lymph nodes removed, again, lots of scar tissue which has caused limited movement. The amazing reconstruction that I had after a double mastectomy has also caused more restrictions. The procedure, used my own tissue taken from my tummy, the whole of the front of my body was opened up (DIEP was the operation). I have a hip to hip scar, the cut went through all the layers of my abdominal muscles. As a result, I have lost 20% of the function of one side of my rectus abdominus and have lost a lot of feeling in my torso. I can't feel my muscles activating. I have to imagine them working to wake them up. When they do work, it is for literally a few moments, then they just stop. This is not a moan, I am so grateful as the surgeons weren't sure what my mobility and strength would be like. My body, as always has exceeded all of my expectations. I am in awe of my body and the skill of the surgeons, and forever grateful.

With all of this in mind, you might think that I am crazy to go to a headstand and handstand yoga workshop. In a physical sense right now, my body can't achieve either of these postures, that is my reality and my truth. However, I went, and not just to one, to lots. I took part in many day long challenging yoga workshops, all with some yoga asanas,(12) that my body physically can't do, but lots that I could do.

I could do something. Not everything that was taught, but something.

I could do the prep work to open and strengthen my body.

I could keep hope.

I could work towards something just for the pure experience and joy of, instead of pinning my worth on the value of doing something purely to attain a goal.

In these workshops, I spent time with my friends and dear teachers. I felt joy. I learnt to detach from the ego's belief that I am complete only when I achieve something. I lived for joy. I chose wisely for myself. I was lit up. I gained strength. I learnt a lot of things and had mini achievements along the way. Can I do a handstand years later? No, but I will never stop trying. I use a wall, to build my arms up as a support and get the sensation of the inversion.

Does this define my worth? Not to me. It could have done though, if I believed in the "I can't," more than the "I choose."

With my workouts, I can't physically do a full press up, I choose to go as far as I can with my knees on the floor. I do something. I don't give in to the first "I can't," or other *'reasons not to'* that come into my head. The "I can't," the *'reasons not to'* that we all default too, by nature of being human. Often, we go into the *'reasons not too,'* because something might be hard, or we might be scared that we will fail.

Instead of "I can't" in these situations, I choose to say, "let's see" "what if"? This changes everything for me. Curiosity instead of expectation to me feels like freedom, compassion and love. How does this feel for you? Would speaking like this to yourself change anything?

I so wish that this resonates and you get a semblance of the a-has that I did, and some thoughts about where you could start to choose you more, to take your power back.

The process that I am going to share with you, really helped me to see with clarity.

In your journal or workbook, divide the paper into 2 sections. On the first side, list all your reasons that you tend to give as to why you can't do things. We all have our own default catchphrases. This could include things that you love, or that you really want to do, and things that you don't like doing.

On the other side, write down whether any of these are true or not.

Take the beliefs one at a time and write down what you could choose to do, if you don't just say "I can't." How does it feel to take this sovereignty back?

Is there any area of your life, any situations or trauma like the first arrow, that life has provided you with? Write them out, give them the space to be seen.

Are there any areas of your life where you are shooting the second arrow? No judgement, lots of compassion. Could you choose a different response? How would it feel to not have the second arrow causing more suffering?

Fear and doubt I honour you

Thank you for keeping me safe
Unseen and hidden
Until I was ready
Trust, faith, passion and purpose
I see you, I feel you, I honour you
I feel and hear your calling
I feel your support
Fear and doubt you must be tired now
Lets let go together
And fall into love
Surrender into trust

CHAPTER NINE
THEY

I wonder if there is one person in this world that hasn't referenced the mythical 'they'?

So many of us, give our power away to this concept of 'they' as an external authority in our lives, dictating and shaping our behaviour.

I certainly was under the spell of 'they' for most of my life. I still catch myself reverting to this state occasionally. I always smile when I catch myself, and remember my beautiful humanness.

"They said we can't."

"They said we must."

"They said we should."

"They said that we are allowed."

A few years ago, I got a very clear loud question in my head, as a response to something someone said to me. "Who the f**k, are they?" It felt like a voice was screaming inside of my head.

I want to pass this question onto you. In your world, "Who the f**k, are they?"

It became very prevalent during the pandemic, that the inconsistencies of what 'they' we're saying defied all reason to my very logical brain. I won't go into the politics of it all here. Just to say that when we give our power away without deeper thinking, we lose our sovereignty. In this fast paced world, where are minds are over burdened just with all the things that we have to do to get through the modern day, it is impossible to think about everything in depth. However, some things require us to find our own truth, separate from what everyone around us is quoting 'they' as saying we should do.

Our minds are tools to analyse, to assess what is around us, to get curious, to question, not to be programmed mindlessly and told what to do, or how things are. Questions and curiosity are paths towards our own truth, our own way of seeing this beautiful life that we are living.

Curiosity is essential to our inner freedom and the preservation of our external freedoms.

Like the work that we did with the previous chapter on 'I can't,' please have a play at catching yourself, when you use the word 'they,' or when you hear it in conversation.

Ask yourself, who are 'they'?

Is it valid what 'they' are saying?

Why do 'they' say this, is it true?

For whose benefit is it?

Does what 'they' are saying go against your values, or your heart?

I always ask myself, in my head, when I am in conversation, who are 'they'? Do 'they' make money from this? What is in it for 'them'?

'They' often have interests in manipulating our behaviour, often in terms of political compliance and consumerism. 'They' can also use this term against the free thinkers, the truth seekers and the souls who question. It can be used to turn citizen upon citizen.

As I write this, it is August 2022, as a mother, I hold fear. I am scared, for the beings that live on this beautiful planet. As an aside, I am not scared for mother earth, she is so wise and adaptable and will keep changing and evolving. The changes that she makes to balance herself however, will effect all of the living beings who rely upon her for their home.

I have two children and I fear for their future with the human enhanced climate change that is happening, and also the polarity that still exists between humans. With all of the labels that we give each other, attached to the country's that we live in, the religions that we practise, or not, the wages that we earn, or not, the colour of our skin, our gender(s), the size of our bodies etc, we seem to have forgotten that we are all sisters and brothers, on this planet together. There is so much polarity, duality and division. I hope in my lifetime, or very soon, enough people remember that we are in this together, not against each other.

I have seen since the start of the pandemic in the UK, a very underhand erosion of human rights and civil liberties.

I studied Law at bachelor level and have a masters in Law specialising in Human Rights and Civil Liberties. Every time my daughter came to me worried about a potential bill that would be passed, in my mind, I remembered my studies of jurisprudence, and reassured her that it couldn't possibly happen. It did, slowly but surely, and often some of the public, felt it was justified, by how protesters, labelled as 'they' have been portrayed by the powers that be.

Taking one example, there was a group of souls demonstrating (I won't go into specific names) using civil disobedience, disrupting the M25, to be heard by the government, to ask that they concentrate on insulating homes for the families that are having to choose between heating or feeding their families. Insulating homes also makes a massive effect on reducing carbon emissions.

I heard 'they' mentioned so much. How dare 'they' disrupt our economy for the day? There were lots of comments, lots of backlash. This backlash, enabled the government to pass acts that severely eroded the right to protest, with relative ease.

When we are sold the concept of 'they,' we have little consideration, that one day, the government might do something that goes so deeply against our own values. That their actions might feel so deeply unjust to us, that one day, we might want to use our own voices, make some noise, stand in our power and exercise our human rights. To someone then, we would become a part of 'they.'

Let's look behind 'they'.

In this instance, 'they' are a group of souls coming from the heart, putting their freedom in danger (often arrests happen, which has a massive effect on the protestors lives.) 'They' are speaking up on behalf of all of us, for all of our benefit, they are going against the norms, they are individuals.

The same with the members of climate protest groups. I have spent some time in London at protests. I spoke to a lot of people also protesting. There were many retired teachers, doctors and nurses. A married couple I spent a while with, were specifically and intentionally there with the aim to get arrested. As retired teachers, they wanted to speak up for all of the children that they had taught, and for their own children and grandchildren. They told me, how they wanted to do something for the future generations. They told me that they have lived an amazing life, and they want to do this for the children of the world. They were not happy about the erosion of civil rights happening in this supposed democracy. No violence would be involved, just standing in their truth and their power. I can still picture her face, her eyes so vivid, alive and sparkling, full of purpose. She was aiming for her first arrest, her husband had already been taken in once.

Often, when we term groups 'they' we don't actually know the story behind why 'they' are doing what 'they' are doing, why 'they' feel so passionate about their cause, who 'they' are as individuals. 'They' tends to objectify 'them'. It is easier to hate on 'them,' when you see them as a mass, not as individual beings, and especially not as retired teachers and grandparents.

My intention for this chapter is to invite you to start to look deeper. Every time you say 'they,' ask yourself, who are 'they'? What are 'they' really doing? Is it really helpful, or is it control?

Choose to take your power back amazing soul, make your own empowered choices, be the wonderful free thinker that you are at your core.

Slowly, piece by piece, decipher and recode the programs running through your head. Move towards standing stronger, taller, more centred and freer in yourself.

I feel so much gratitude and hope flowing from my heart. Thank you for being here at this time, for clicking the button to order this book. Thank you for being open. Thank you for being you. That action matters and you matter.

Now a pause for contemplation if you choose. In your journal or notebook, record when you say 'they,' or when you hear it and do some investigation.

In your world, who are 'they'?

I Give Up

I've decided to give up, to surrender
I know it bothers you
You'd prefer me to keep quiet anyway
To not rock the boat
It's just that it's becoming too painful for me to care
About the animals
My children
Their children
Their children's children
And Mother Earth
I give up
I just want to be okay in this moment
I want to surround myself with comfort
With all the things I like doing
Got to look after number one don't we?
Thats what I hear
It's so hard to take responsibility for my own life
To lead myself with a clear conscience
I'm just going to crawl under the blanket of ignorance again
Beautiful, blissful ignorance
Unaware of whats true for future generations
As long as we are okay now
When it all happens, I will have nearly lived my life
At least I will be okay
When my children ask me why
Why I didn't do things to help
I'll remind them that they had

All they had ever wanted
That we looked after ourselves
Thats all we could do
I'll talk to them about how what we do
doesn't matter
We don't count
We are voiceless
We are victims
We are not like those souls creating civil
disobedience
What a waste of time
What a waste of our money hey?
I'll remind them, that they can't cause change
That they will just have to accept their lot
You see, when I care
It means that I have a choice
A hope of change
It feels too much, too hard
One minute I have hope
The next minute I am lost
If I choose to tread lightly on this beautiful
earth
I will need to keep learning
And refining
Maybe let go of some luxuries
Maybe ruffle some feathers
If I choose to connect deeply
With the world around me
It will cost me time and effort
In this moment I have all that I need
So I am going to choose not to care
I choose the easiest path right now
I will just blame everyone else

I'll join in with everyone else's distaste of the rebels
I'll moan about how they cost the economy some money for that day
And caused inconvenience
While I am in this space
Whilst I have your attention
I will shout at all the peaceful activists
Those heart centred souls
Who dedicate and devote themselves
To our freedom, wellness and home (mother earth)
I will tell them not to bother
They are just too much of an inconvenience
To my life, and I know yours too
They are causing too much disruption
Yes, I will give up
I will give up taking responsibility for my own wellness
I'll hand it over to the other
To them
I'll stop investing time and care in myself
I'll take the pills
I'll give up freeing my mind of limiting beliefs
I'll give up stepping into my power
It's just too much
I'll go back to playing small and hiding
It is so much easier there
You don't get criticised then
You don't feel compelled to take action
Yes, thats what I'll do
I'll start numbing my mind

I'll dull down
I'll stop feeling into life in its fullest
expression
Because it really hurts when I do
I'll stop growing
Yep, thats me
Giving up…

Will I f**k

CHAPTER TEN
DESERVE & LUCKY

This is a word that caught me off guard recently when I used it. It triggered a physical feeling of sickness in my body, it repulsed me. So I stopped and contemplated the word and my use of it.

It was a word that I used a lot and I still catch myself saying, I haven't quite reprogrammed yet. I used to say it to myself, to my friends, family, to my clients and students.

"Yes, take a break, you deserve it."

"No, of course not, you didn't deserve that kind of treatment, thats awful."

There are many other sayings with the word deserve woven in. So many sayings that we have all picked up. I decided there and then to stop using it, it is still very much a work in progress. I am still in the de-conditioning phase. That word is part of the tapestry of language and phraseology that I have heard and used all of my life.

A reminder, that you matter, you're thoughts about yourself, your thoughts about others matter and the words that you speak out into the world matter. The words you speak are your thoughts manifested into the world. Your words are your unique creative expression that is woven into the fabric of the universe.

I was so enchanted when I learnt, what 'Abracadabra' means. It literally sent shivers through all of the cells in my body. It illuminated and bound so many of my thoughts together, into a massive lightbulb moment.

Abracadabra means "I will create as I speak."

Our speech is our manifestation. How amazing is that? A power to use wisely, with heart, with conscious intention, with love and compassion.

The thoughts and words that we choose to use, affect the flow of energy in our body, our vibrational state and the way that our DNA is expressed. (This is the science of epigenetic's which I won't venture into here.) This affects our wellness on so many levels. This is the reason I started my own personal journey, to be super clear and pure with my thoughts, to strip them back to my values, to strip them back to love.

I believe that it doesn't matter whether we just think the words, or speak them out loud, the other feels them, and our cells feel the energy of them. In quantum physics, and in the ancient cultures, at source, there is 'no other.' We belong to one collective consciousness. In the ancient philosophies, we live our earth walk in our separate bodies until we go back to the whole. We are so interconnected. Science has now proven that quantum entanglement is real. It blows my mind, every time I learn about the quantum field. Science is literally proving what the original and ancient cultures believed and lived according to, to be true. I am not going into detail in this book on the subject of quantum physics, if you feel the pull, it is so worth researching and learning more about.

I believe that others can feel the energy of you through a text, an email, a zoom meeting or recording. Our energy transcends the physical. I know that I can feel this. I have felt others expressions, emotions and intentions through these means of connection. Which is what in effect they are, an energetic connection, communication through the ether. If someone is feeling negative in themselves or towards me, I feel their energy as a blow to my solar plexus, sometimes so forceful, that it makes me recoil and takes my breath away.

The last time I remember saying the words deserve, I was saying to a client, "Yes, thats brilliant, you so deserve that." The moment the words left my mouth, it felt horrendous, it felt so wrong to say it. I noted my reaction. I have trained my brain to be aware of my words, and the impact that they have upon my energy. I made a note to investigate it, to contemplate why I had that reaction.

This is the definition of deserve from Oxford Languages, (13) do something or have or show qualities worthy of (a reaction which rewards or punishes as appropriate).

Ahh, that was why.

So, at its core essence, the word means that you have to do something, or own something that another being or institution deems worthy of a reaction. The reaction, the determination of worth comes from the external, taking it a little further, someone else gets to determine whether what you deserve is negative or positive.

Nope, not into that. I'm not allowing the opinion of others determine what I am worthy of. It's been years of work to try and bring myself back to feeling enough. I know it's not just me. I see the whole of society so fragile with our sense of worth, with all the measurements, the comparisons, the social pressure that we get pressed upon us and bombarded with.

We are all capable of amazing things, wonderful things can happen, in our lives, and horrible things happen, too. We can all do things that aren't very nice, we can all do things that don't work out. We experiment, we make mistakes, we have wild first time successes. That is the nature of life and it should be, without another label being attached to it, without someone judging what our actions 'deserve.'

Do you deserve something, or is it just part of your path, part of learning, part of life?

Did I deserve cancer?

Was it dished out to me because I was naughty once?

This in essence for me, feels what the word 'deserve' in our modern day world is being used for. It feels to me like another form of judgement. It also feels like everything is judged.

Going back to the definition, who is there to judge who deserves what? It sounds like a system where somebody is higher than another. I don't believe that anyone is above me anymore. I used to think and feel that I was below others, that I wasn't as worthy as other people around me. I will speak about this more in chapter thirteen.

In order to fully heal this collective wound, in order to stop giving our self-agency, belief and worth away to others, to be measured by various numbers and words, we first, have to accept our enough-ness. It is essential.

By the nature of measuring another persons worth against my own, with standards that society holds dear, if I place myself below another, by nature, this also means that I will place myself above another. My study of yogic philosophy illuminated this belief that I was holding. I chose to let my ego soften around this. I chose to feel enough, so that I could escape this man made comparison of someone being better than someone else. I chose to believe that we are all beautiful perfect light, there is no one better than the other. This is challenging for the ego. I still slip. I catch myself. I remind myself that I am beautifully human and I reset.

I hear all around me, and I am so aware that I was fully in the conversations, that go something like this, both internally and externally.

"I am better because I work really hard and earn £1,000 an hour. They only earn £10 an hour."

"They do this … they think that, so they don't deserve this, they deserve that, I deserve this."

"I know they were a bit outspoken but they didn't deserve that treatment."

Can you hear the tones of judgement, the layers of what is better? This is how the ego works, this is how society has tried to separate us, this capitalist hierarchical system that we have been born into.

I believed it for a while, I was in, it was all I had known. Until I saw the programming, until I learnt that our mind is naturally created to judge. To calculate who is safe to be around, who will be helpful for the tribe, essential for survival back in the cave days. Although the primitive brain hasn't moved on, and still behaves like this. I believe that our consciousness is capable of evolving, our ability not to give into the ego has increased, if we take the time to be aware and believe in our own power.

As I reprogrammed, I began to trust, to deeply believe and feel, that we are not separate. We are all beautiful beings of light, all wanting love, to be seen, heard and respected. As a collective, we have moved so far away from source that we feel lost, disconnected and so separate from each other.

I have written this book, because I believe that the words that we use either take us further away from our true nature, or help us remember and step back into love. The words we use can keep us in a separate polarised state of being or unite us.

In the capitalist centric cultures that we live in, it is so challenging to feel whole, to feel enough. The systems and structures around us are geared for setting us up to feel disconnected.

When we forget our interconnectedness, we feel alone, we feel so separate from others. My hope for you reading this book is that you start to feel the pull back, the calling to heal, for yourself, your family and the collective.

As I am still reprogramming and de-conditioning myself, I still catch myself going to say the word deserve.

It is the little things, like "You've done a lot of work today, you deserve to put your feet up."

When I notice, I scream in my head, "No."

You can stop and put your feet up whenever you want. You don't need to have exerted a certain amount of effort first. You can just be, without having to have earned the right or the worth, to have a rest. Really sit with this, can you feel the conditioning underneath it all? The levels of subservience?

Let's have a deeper look at the question, that actually did go through my head at the time. Did I deserve cancer? I was told time after time that I didn't deserve it, these words really stuck with me.

Because I was told that I didn't deserve cancer, does that mean that in some instances I could have deserved cancer? That someone else might have deserved cancer? Just a thought to leave with you.

Did I demonstrate qualities that were worthy of the reaction that my body had in order to make cancer? I am pretty sure, as I take responsibility that something, or many things I did caused my body to let a rogue cell get out of hand. Who knows? Even if a doctor could pinpoint it, and say, you know when you did that, thats when the cancer started. That did it. Even if it could be proven that it was my doing, "you deserved to get cancer," doesn't feel very good to a cancer patient or a survivor. It induces feelings of guilt, shame, judgement, self flagellation, not enoughness and so many more different thoughts, beliefs and emotions, none of them positive, or helpful for healing.

The first time I was diagnosed, when I was in victim mode, I lamented to myself, "why me?" I asked myself this, over and over again.

"What did I do to deserve this?" I can remember saying to my yoga tutor, "I must have been really bad in my past life to deserve this." We were studying the concept of Karma for the yogic philosophy module at the time.

When I was in victimhood the first time, it was like it had been dished out to me, I didn't have any control over it. The second time I took complete ownership. This happened to me, it might have just happened anyway, but from my understanding of epigenetic's, maybe the birth control tablet I was on for years since the age of 14 (for an acne treatment) was a problem, or perhaps the way I handled my emotions, as in not asking for help, keeping everything suppressed, bottling it all up, being a massive people pleaser, having no self worth at all, ignoring the calling of my soul, maybe all that mattered?

Perhaps the years of partying that I enjoyed so much mattered, perhaps not. It could have been all the toxins I used in hair and skin care products, especially the perfume that disrupted my endocrine system and tipped my body over the edge?

Who knows?

The second time, I didn't think, well, I deserved that. But I did accept that I have some power over my future. I went on a journey of self discovery and healing. I started to listen to the me before I got programmed by life.

What gives me joy?

Who am I?

What am I here for?

How can I use this experience positively?

How can I use it to grow and transform?

I want to utilise this suffering for a reason. I believe I have been through this experience for reason.

What do I do with that?

I slowly started to look at my beliefs, and find me again. I searched and found my own light, that was buried underneath all the should's, the labels, the programming.

I started to talk to myself like someone I love. I

remembered that it is okay to love myself.

To love yourself is essential, it should not mean that I am cocky or arrogant. In the UK, if someone is doing well and is confident, owning their power and the people around them aren't, they often get talked about, the fingers point at them, and things like "Look at them, who do they think they are?" "They so love themselves" are said. This infiltrates our psyche. If I love myself I am arrogant, if I see my light and brilliance, people will think I am cocky.

How sad is this?

It can hold us back if we allow it to, from enjoying and owning our skills and our talents, worrying about what others think and say.

I get drawn to people who recognise and own their strengths and talents. These are the people that I choose as my inspiration, teachers and guides. Not someone who is blending in and playing small. I seek out as a guide, someone who can light the path that I am ready to walk.

For this reason, I choose to shine and be there for the souls who are ready to walk with me.

I used to talk to myself with such negativity, such self-loathing. I did not honour my body, the temple that my soul resides in for this earth walk. I didn't get mad with myself when I realised. I held myself in a compassionate state, and just kept on steadily healing one thing after the other.

Now I am in the process of removing the word deserve from my vocabulary. I reject the way that is used in modern day society, this idea that someone else has authority over what I deserve, and that I have the power to dictate this to someone else. Everything goes both ways.

This doesn't feel sovereign to me. This feels like someone else has authority over me. I am here for my own personal power, not power over anyone else. That second form of power is a false power. It is domination over the other, not personal power. My definition of personal power, is when you know who you are, you feel connected to your sense of worth, you own your uniqueness and honour all parts and aspects of you. Because of this, you are full of your own essence, you feel complete, you feel enough, and you don't feel the need to put others down, or to dominate anyone else to temporarily feel better about yourself.

The more I contemplated, the more toxic this word felt, it had so many different layers that repelled me.

It felt that in order to 'deserve' there is often a large amount of effort, hustle, grind, grit and hardship involved, to get the accolade of deserving.

What about, if two people get to the same end result. The first person got there with pure determination, push energy and hustle. The second person rested a lot to manage their energy, had massive self belief, trust in themselves, trust in the universe, the path to that goal was effortless and easeful? For the second person, the right thing at the right time seemed to just magically happen.

What if they both got to a goal at the same time but in completely different ways? The hustle path would be crowned as deserving the end result, the second success would most be likely termed as lucky.

Society, films, books, stories, our culture, honours the struggle, the heroes journey, against all the odds. These kinds of journeys are so inspiring. I do love a good hero's tale. I love to remember the resilience of humans and to remind myself that anything is possible, when I see someone overcome all obstacles.

The soul who got there with ease, they did work too. They did the work of surrender, trusting, of tuning into and soothing their nervous system, reconnecting with their intuition, being conscious of the choices that they make, the people and opportunities around them. They were present, which is so challenging. They kept their focus, they kept on their path, they were committed to healing. They probably had to deal with a lot of comments about how it couldn't be that easy. A lot of work in the unseen. Is that any less valuable? And who determines what is valuable anyway?

Why all this competition between us all?

Does that soul deserve it any less? I will leave that question open for you, what does your conditioning tell you? It will be there. I am still deconstructing my beliefs that I have held all my life. From giving kudos to the struggle to get somewhere, that success is a challenge, that it can't possibly be that easy, that it must be earned with blood, sweat and tears.

I work super quickly, I get an idea, some inspiration, and just get into action. I am able to create in a short amount of time, it's just how I work. It feels easy to me because I have done the self development work. I know who I am, and I commit my energy to my souls purpose, and what brings me joy. However, with most of the projects that I undertake, in the background, before I feel the inspiration to create, I have spent hours learning, building the systems, gaining the skills that I will need for potential projects. Refining my mind to be able to work in this way. Programming myself to believe that I can. Soothing my nervous system, to stop going into a flight or freeze response which could potentially stop me doing and taking action.

But this, the background work is not seen. I sometimes get told that everything is easy for me. It might appear that way on the outside. Who knows what is easy or a struggle for anyone else? We just don't. All we can know for sure is how we are experiencing our lives, what is feeling easy, or challenging for ourselves.

Shouldn't we aim for ease?

Why aim for struggle when we have the option of aligned purposeful and easeful action?

When I opened my yoga studio, I got told how lucky I was. Was I lucky? I took a risk, I chose to go way outside of my comfort zone, I chose to borrow money, there was no luck with it, just aligned inspired action. At the time, I agreed. I thought I was lucky, because I was following my joy, I did feel lucky.

The fact that I was having fun and enjoying myself appeared to invalidate both for myself and others what I was actually doing. It wasn't being considered as actual 'work.' I noticed that there is an underlying concept that work shouldn't be enjoyable. I observed that if I was enjoying something, especially as a female, people were labelling it as a 'hobby' or a 'little business'. Another wow.

In reality though, I was constantly challenging myself, taking massive risks and taking constant aligned action with many hours of work and effort. I had to learn so many new things. I wasn't acknowledging my own drive, personal power and commitment, by just thinking that I was lucky.

When we don't recognise our own power, when we give it away to societies ideals and the praise of others, when we don't honour ourselves, we see everyone else who we deem successful as lucky. To acknowledge that others work hard, or the fact that they created their own reality, means that we would have to look within, to believe that we have this ability too, and then choose what to do about it.

The brain loves us to stay small, tucked safely away inside our comfort zone. Even if we are not happy, it takes great belief, trust and strength to grow to the edges of your comfort zone. Let alone, progress to the other side of it. This is called the neuro-set point. I am constantly dedicated to expanding my own. I do not want to stagnate in this lifetime. I want to feel my brilliance, I want to transform. I want to express my souls purpose with clarity.

Let's take a deeper dive into the concept of luck, as it is so interwoven with deserve, in our society. It feels like you either deserve something or you are lucky.

I want to caveat again, that this book is an expression of my lens of perception, of how I view certain things in the world. My perception is ever changing, this book is an expression of where I am now, how I am processing my thoughts in the year 2022, what I believe will be helpful to express into the world at this present time. This book is a way of gently inviting you to come to your truth, to delve into your beliefs and see what is there.

I also want to acknowledge the white privilege that I have had throughout my whole life, by being born into a white body in the UK. The topic of systemic racism is so insidious and vast, so interwoven into the global community, I could not do it justice here. If you have never looked at your white privilege, please start to look deeper. If the mere phrase triggers you, please look deeper. It is essential that the deep colonial and racist shadows that have created the structures, communities and ways of thinking and being, be called out into the light. However uncomfortable that may feel. It matters.

Before I took radical responsibility for myself, I used to look at people who had what my ego desired, or the souls who had achieved the goal that I wanted, with green tinted eyes, with jealousy. I had thoughts such as…

"It's okay for them, they are so lucky."

"Of course they got there, they had a head start."

"Things always turn out okay for them."

"They always land on their feet."

These are a few, there were many, many more. I was in such a victim mentality. I did not believe that I had much worth in this world, and I certainly didn't think that I could achieve anything that I wanted. I had created a strong mental construct, a box to contain my possibility within.

Slowly, over time, the call of my soul, the whisper that I mattered got louder and louder from within. I started to consider the possibility that I have incarnated here, at this time for a reason. Eventually, I heard it. I started to take responsibility, I started to get inspired by the souls that I once used to feel jealousy towards.

I truly believe, and I hope this resonates deep inside of you, that when you do feel envious, or look up to someone else, it is because those qualities that you see in them, are within you. Those feelings are an acknowledgment of a deep energetic resonance that you share with that being.

There is a female entrepreneur that I admire. She has activist tendencies, she loves wellness and she is wildly successful in her business. I caught myself thinking, that's okay for her, she started early, she was there at the 'right time.' Then, I realised that she was a mirror. I had all of that inside of me. I just didn't have the self belief or worth. Because I was lacking belief, I wasn't taking the aligned steps that my soul was crying out for.

From that moment on, if I feel jealousy creeping in, or the "It's okay for them," I catch it, I love myself for forgetting my power and I remind myself of my beautiful humanness.

I get inspired instead.

I get inquisitive.

What is it that I love about the way they show up?

What resonates with me?

What would I do differently, if I was where they are?

I have been on the receiving end of the you are so lucky comments, and I guarantee, I am not above or below anyone else. I have taken aligned action and am always working on my healing and belief.

Looking at starting my yoga studio, as an illustration, here is a little run down of what it took for me to open my own studio. I listened to my souls purpose, which has taken different expressions over time. At the beginning of my yoga teaching journey, it was born from pure awe at the power that yoga had upon my body and nervous system. The wonderment of how amazing and connected it helped me feel. I simply wanted to share this. I wanted to help as many people as I could feel the way that I did, it was like sharing medicine for the soul.

This is part of my soul's purpose, my essence, I am here to share what I love, what I am passionate about. So I signed up for the teacher training. I wanted to teach yoga, I was so excited. On the first day, the tutor asked us to introduce ourselves and why we were here. I was the only one in the class, who said explicitly, "I want to be a yoga teacher." I had taken ownership. I was intentional. I had belief. I had invested my time, money and energy. I had belief in the tutors, and the calling of my soul. Belief in yourself is so important, along with aligned action. That course was 500 hours plus more study and practise. I was dedicated. When friends were partying, or my family was out at the weekends, I was studying and training.

When it came to teaching, that's when I had to dig deep again. I had to believe even more. I chose to put myself out there and teach 2 years of yoga classes before I could get my qualification. I was in the middle of the first breast cancer episode and was on hormone treatment which made my weight balloon. I felt so uncomfortable in my own skin, and I had a limiting belief that kept popping up. I certainly didn't feel enough, my sense of self esteem was so low. I truly believed, that no one would take me seriously as I wasn't a size 8 and didn't have long legs. Yes, this is what my fearful mind deemed important in a yoga teacher, I knew that I was a good yoga teacher, so it had to find some other ways that I was lacking. I had to keep digging so deep to find some worth, to remember my purpose, to get into aligned action. That is not easy, that takes so much mental and emotional energy, and daily energetic practises to keep my vibration high. It also took reaching out, putting myself out there, but I did it. I set up five very successful yoga classes, and worked at gyms with fully booked classes. My sense of purpose, my desire to share with others was greater than '*any reason not to.*'

That wasn't luck.

I made that happen.

I had the inspired idea and vision of creating my own space for just me to teach yoga in, calm, clean, warm, nurturing, with props and blankets to really nourish my students. Three weeks later it happened. I invested money, time and energy. I had to ask for help to get the studio ready. I took a chance. I didn't have an income for a long time, to break even. I was told that it was risky, why are you doing that, you are okay, your classes are working. Again, belief, inspired action. There was no luck. So many limiting beliefs and fears about what people would think of me popped up. "Who am I to get a yoga studio?" I held space for them and let them move. I just kept coming back to my body and feeling into my passion.

Behind every 'successful' person, is someone stretching themselves way outside of their comfort zone, committed to their personal growth, listening to their souls calling, taking aligned and probably very scary action. Choosing to tune out the people around them who are trying to keep them safe by staying where they are, tuning out the haters, redirecting the envious energy pointed their way. Pausing occasionally to let their nervous system recalibrate. Choosing to have daily practises to keep their energy high vibe, trusting in themselves and the universe. As I have mentioned, often a lot goes on in the unseen, this is the internal work.

The beautiful thing, is that this is all possible for you, if you listen to your heart. What is it you really want? It could be that you want to paint at the weekend, or dance more. It doesn't have to be a life changing risky business move. Just what would you love to do more of? Then start to heal your limiting beliefs and take action.

How do you view others success when it seems easeful?

Do you ever think it's okay for them, that they are different to you, that they are lucky?

I used to and still catch, myself sometimes. I am a beautiful fragile human with a mind that does this. I just keep remembering time and time again, my values and beliefs and find my way back to my centre and my truth.

A space for contemplation.

How has this chapter resonated with you?

What beliefs did you have around the words lucky and deserve?

Do you use them how I did?

How do you feel about them now?

What has changed?

Do you believe that you can create your own reality?

Now, to create another JOY List. I hope that finding joy will be easier for you now, after you initial investigation in the previous chapter. You are allowed so much joy in your life beautiful soul, it is your birth right.

Divide your paper into two halves.

On the first, write down all the things that bring you joy, from childhood to present, these could be the little things and the bigger things. Add on to the list, all the things that you would like to do for joy, not for a goal, just for the sheer joy of doing it.

Look at the list, note in the second column which ones you can do more of now, in this 3D version of reality that you are living in right now. In the second column note how you could start to introduce more of those things into your life, and also plan to do some of the things on your list.

This isn't a bucket list, it is about consciously making your everyday infused with more joy.

For example, I love cacao ceremonies, so I hold my own for myself every morning! More joy.

<u>I honour the light in you…</u>

What does that really mean?
It starts with YOU
It starts when YOU honour the light in YOU
Everything you see in this lifetime including other beings
Is a reflection of what is inside of YOU

CHAPTER ELEVEN
FINE

Another word that stood out to me, that sparked me to look a little deeper and observe the use of it. Fine, of very high quality; very good of its kind. "this was a fine piece of film-making", very thin or narrow, "a fine nylon thread" fine; very small particles found in mining, milling, etc, in a satisfactory or pleasing manner; very well." "And how's the job-hunting going?" "Oh, fine."(15)

I have observed that 'fine,' tends to be used as a throw away word, something to hide behind. At the start of my weekly Yin classes, I ask my students how they are, with the invitation to not use the words, 'fine', 'good', or 'OK'. To guide them into the depth of the emotions that they have inside themselves to be seen and felt.

When I ask someone how they are, my spider senses tingle whenever someone replies 'fine'. It either tends to mean that they don't think I really want to know how they are. That they feel I am just being polite and using a socially acceptable greeting. For me personally, I don't ask questions that I don't care about the answer to anymore. I used to, I was so into the social protocol, just regurgitating what I had heard all around me. If I am not genuinely interested, I don't ask. Do you?

Sometimes 'fine,' means that they can't be bothered to go into it, or maybe they don't actually know how they feel, or how they are. Quite often, it means that they are not okay at all, but don't want to burden me, or that they feel amazing and don't want to feel like they are boasting. This happens a lot doesn't it? Self depreciation, dimming our light so as to not upset people who aren't lit up, who aren't feeling so good. When I am not in a good space, I find those beings that are shining inspiring, they are my positivity, they are my light to help guide me back.

We all need more light in our lives.

Be the light.

Shine.

I noticed something deep within the English culture, when I started to decondition myself. There is this underlying sense, that we shouldn't be 'too good.' That there should be an undercurrent of not quite being okay. That people might resent us if we share about how amazing we feel, we could come across as a show off.

We are programmed to blend in. To not make a fuss. We should be okay, but not "grand" as my beautiful Irish friends say. Have you noticed this too. "How are you?" "Oh you know middling," "OK, " "Hanging in there," so many typical socially acceptable responses have this tone of bearing with, just about getting by. Like it is the norm to not feel good, as though it is normal to be in a state of mild to intense suffering.

I observed in myself first and then in others, that if I was feeling good, or something was going well, I did play it down, so as not to come across as 'bragging'. Especially if I could feel that the soul in front of me wasn't feeling so good.

I would consciously lower my vibration, in order to match theirs. I would hide my joy, hide my light, not celebrate, or let them know the wonderful things that were happening in my life. I believed that this was necessary in order to help them feel better about themselves. This all came from my ego of course. My perception and assumption of how they were really feeling and what I believed that they needed from me. None of this is actually my business unless the other chooses to share how they are feeling with me. This is a lesson that took me so long to learn. I still get triggered and still fall into hiding.

Now I aim to be the joy, to share my love, my light. To remind souls with my inner peace and happiness, that the state that they are in will pass. That the beautiful emotion of joy is available to them. I believe in the power of resonance, that by vibrating at this level, others around me, in the unconscious will start to raise their vibration. (Quantum Physics again.)

Choose to be the light beautiful soul, it will help others remember theirs. It is always there within, it just gets forgotten sometimes.

When you ask someone how they are, do you really care how they are? If I don't, if I see someone I know in the street, but we aren't close, I will say "Hi." If I have a connection, if I have a relationship with you, I will ask you how you are, because, I really want to know how you are. I care. I want to hear your reply.

Like 'overwhelm,' 'fine,' feels like a blanket to cover up

our feelings. It is acceptable, widely used, very beige, not offensive in any way. It doesn't reveal much about how we are doing.

What does 'fine' mean to you?

If you look at the official definition, there isn't really any mention of emotions. So why do we use it when we are replying to someone asking us how we are?

With some friends and clients, I ask, how is your heart, how is your soul, how are you truly doing? We are designed as humans to care about each other, to have deep soulful communication. Yet, it seems that society likes to keep it at surface level, nice and clean. Emotions aren't always convenient to have. They can be a bit messy can't they? They can make others feel uncomfortable. Maybe even for ourselves, to sometimes really be truthful about how we feel, can feel out of control, raw, tender and so intense. If we can't hold space for our own free flow of emotions, how can we hold the space for others?

As a rule, we aren't taught emotional intelligence at school, (although I am happy to see this is changing). In effect, by it's omission, we are programmed to deny our own. Hence a society, that uses the words like 'fine,' with a stiff upper lip. As a nation, I am talking about the UK here. I really do believe that in general we are emotionally repressed.

What I have seen a lot, is that some of the beautiful souls who come for sessions with me are disconnected, and numb to their own emotions. Adrift from the language to describe how they are feeling. Numb from automatically responding "Fine" and "OK" or whatever response is coded into their programming.

I encourage my clients to look at a list of emotional words and choose how they are feeling from this list. At first this is such a challenge, but it gets easier. I can remember when I started this work, I had an underlying tone of deep sadness. I didn't know it was there as I kept everything surface level. As I tuned back into myself and reconnected with my emotions, I allowed them to be seen and acknowledged. To be held, to be expressed, to be honoured. One by one, I faced them and felt them. I mentioned in an earlier chapter that the emotions feel intense, but they will pass, they have to. It might feel as though the wave of emotion might engulf you, as though it might physically take your breath away. It might for a time, but the water will subside and the whelm will pass.

You will breathe deeply again and your calm will return.

Awareness in its own right is so healing, so empowering, this is how we take our power back. Without knowing how we are feeling and how we are truly doing, we stumble through life, on autopilot. By default, agreeing and submitting to the systems. We are dumbing our lights down, not letting ourselves feel, stagnating the flow of energy and just creating an inner sense of being off, not quite right. It can be very subtle, we don't always notice it. When this happens, we are not in an energetic position to feel enough as ourselves, or to believe in our own uniqueness and begin to take the steps on our path of aligned action. When we come back into our power, when we align, everyone around us feels it, it ripples outwards.

Some people around us might not like it when we change. It can be triggering to see someone grow, as it highlights our own stagnation, fears, and unfulfilled desires. The soul that is growing and stepping into their own light and expansiveness is a mirror, reflecting back to us where we are stuck. Illuminating our souls desires. The desires that we are ignoring.

As you heal, as you become more conscious of your thoughts, words, and beliefs, be open to resistance from others. Expect change. Welcome it. As you rise, the souls around you that are ready will rise with you. As you find your light, you will shine, so that others can illuminate their shadows and start the process to heal and let their souls evolve. And on it goes. Some people in your life will choose to stay where they are, that is their journey, not yours. Love and accept them for where they are. Release any responsibility for their growth that your ego is holding onto.

You are the change beautiful soul. I believe it. I believe this is why you have this book in your hands, I wish that you start to believe it too.

Often we don't want to shine, or show our happiness in front of others who might be in a place of suffering. I don't know about you, but when I see the Sun, when I see the light, it lifts me up. I don't want everyone around me to suffer just because I am. I want the light. Like a flower, we all instinctively turn our heads towards the light. It makes us feel more alive, more vital.

Be the light.

Be the light for yourself.

Be the light for those around you.

I am going to invite you to be open to this challenge, that I hope with all my heart you take up. When someone asks you how you are, don't say fine anymore, be honest in your response to them.

This will allow you to develop a more honest self awareness, and build a deeper connection with others in your life. It leads to juicier, full bodied, open hearted conversations and connections. Every morning, ask yourself how you are feeling, look at a list of emotions if the words still aren't coming naturally to you. Test them out, speak them out loud.

Practise with people you love, talk to them about your experiment, encourage them to join you.

Write a list of words that feel and sound like you.

Here are some of my responses when people ask how I am, real phrases I have said to my yoga students and friends and family whom I know care about my response.

"I feel really happy today, thank you for asking, what about you?"

"I feel really sad and worried today, my dog hasn't been

very well. But I am still looking forward to teaching you all, you light me up, I love my time with you all."

"You know, I feel really content and peaceful today."

"I feel a bit flat today"

"I feel a bit ungrounded."

"I feel a bit, anxious, a bit nervous today for some reason and I don't know why."

"I feel really excited, I feel like I am bursting with possibility."

"I am in a right mood today, but feel better for seeing you."

This is how I talk, this has helped others around me to open up more, to investigate themselves, to deepen their emotional intelligence and most importantly, deepen their relationship with themselves.

Our number one relationship is with ourselves, and yet I was so disconnected. And I know I wasn't alone in this. When we are suffering, there is the inclination to feel alone, like we are the only ones feeling this way. We are never alone. When I realised this, I was able to soften, to be kinder to myself and hold a deeper level of compassion.

You are never truly alone, even though you might feel it. Question yourself. Are you truly alone, or is it that you are not allowing anyone to help you? Are you donning a warrior woman facade like I did? Are you denying the raw and painful emotions that come with getting honest and vulnerable? You have the strength to be vulnerable beautiful soul.

One of my biggest healings, began with my observation that I felt alone. I was feeling resentful that no-one knew how I was feeling, that no-one was there for me, that I was doing it all alone. This was so far from the truth. I had so many people who cared about me in my life. I just wasn't letting them in emotionally. With the warrior woman cape that I put on everyday to keep myself together, I was stopping my emotions getting out, but also love and support getting in. Boundaries and barriers operate both ways. I was emotionally isolating myself. The remedy came when I softened and opened up to myself first, and then I began to allow others in. I found this so challenging as it went against all of the programs I had in my psyche to cope with life.

I realised that feeling alone in a room with people whom I love and who love me, felt far more lonely than being physically alone. I chose to heal this. None of it was real, it was all the way that I was viewing life, my programming and how I was choosing to be.

When we go through life on autopilot, not being conscious of the words what we use, we can create these situations in our lives. I would have been telling everyone that I was 'fine,' 'good,' and 'okay,' at this stage in my life. I really wasn't. With the use of these words, I was lying to myself and everyone else around me. The words that we use matter.

A time to pause and consider the following prompts.

What are your responses before reading this chapter when someone ask you how you are?

Do you really care about someones response when you ask them how they are?

If not, what could you say instead?

How does this chapter resonate with you?

What other words and phrases could you say instead?

Do you commit to trying the "I am not going to say fine challenge?"

Behind every closed door

Behind every closed door
There is pain
There is suffering
There are things we don't know
Things we will never feel

Behind every fixed smile
Behind every strong mask
There is pain
There is suffering
There are things we don't know

Behind every "I'm fine"
Behind every "I'm okay"
There is pain
There is suffering
There are things we don't know

Inside ourselves
There is pain
There is suffering
There are things we don't know

Inside all those who have hurt us
There is pain
There is suffering
There are things we don't know

We are all hiding
We are all hurt
We are all pretending

Open your heart

Only then can you open your heart to others
Start to connect with others
Start to accept others
See that person who hurt you
Or the person you are judging
Because they appear different to you
As a human with a heart
And a soul that needs healing
With a story full of pain
With a past full of suffering
Who is just trying to get through the day

The person you are looking down on
They want
They deserve
They crave
Respect
Love
Understanding
Just as you do

They could be stuck
They could be sad
They could be arrogant
They could be homeless
They could be fat
They could be thin
They could look like the most beautiful
creature on the earth
We are all the same
We all have self doubt

We all question ourselves
We all crave more connection whether we know it or not
We all wish for unconditional true accepting love

We remember all the criticism
All the times people told us we were not good enough
We hurt ourselves
We eat, exercise and self medicate our feelings away
We become numb
We become disconnected
We get lost

Open your heart
Open your eyes
Remember
Behind every closed door
There is pain
There is suffering
There are things we don't know
Things we will never feel

CHAPTER TWELVE FAILURE, EXPECTATION AND THE MIND

This might sound strange, but I don't think I have ever really said that I have failed much. I tend to say something along the lines of, "Well that didn't go to plan." Or "Hhhmmmm, I learnt a lot there."

I have always loved to feel it all, to have such a wide range of experiences and learn by doing, by experimenting, by living. I have always loved trying new things, I struggle to take instructions in by listening alone, I have to do at the same time to embed the teaching into my psyche. It is my learning style. I try things out in order to learn. So for me, I have simply been learning not failing.

Even if I did use the word 'fail' in my vocabulary, it would be one of the words that I would decondition from and stop using.

From the Oxford Languages - Failure, lack of success, the neglect or omission of expected or required action.(16)

"Failure is defined as a lack of success or the inability to meet an expectation. The problem is that we can read too much into failure. Too often, we tie it to our sense of self-worth, self-esteem, and self-acceptance." (17)

This is a great definition, and exactly why I believe that we can give so much power away to it.

At the root of failure, lies expectation. The expectation

that we will get a desired result, and if we don't get it, we fail. I teach a lot, that our mind's are amazing tools, to conceptualise, to analyse, to filter, to focus, to help us live in this 3D world. But, they are finite, they are limited. They don't know for sure what will happen, they don't know what the final result will be, it is all guess work, or an educated estimate. In most cases, where we end up is unforeseeable. In my experience, I could never have predicted where I am now in my life and business. The journey and outcome so far has been so much more wildly successful, full of the most amazing twists and turns, leading me somewhere far more magical than my limited brain could ever have imagined.

The beautiful mind, that is so useful, is the most amazing tool, yet in modern western society, we give it so much power. When we promote the mind to the status that we have, we take our awareness and authority away from our body, from our gut instinct, from our inner knowing, from nature, from the universal consciousness and from infinite possibilities.

The mind is a tool for processing information that happens in this 3D world, it thinks, it creates concepts based upon our reality. It helps us file information, experiences and make sense of this world. We set filters for it, pertaining as to what it should focus on, (the reticular activating system), so that we can live in relative normalcy, instead of having to notice everything in every moment, as our senses would be completely overloaded. I love the reticular activating system, it allows us to tell our brain what to focus on. If we want a red car, it will log this, and you will see red cars everywhere. If you are feeling really angry, or if more generically, you are attached to feeling angry and complaining, it will draw your attention to so many more things that you can be angry about.

On the opposite side of the spectrum, if you practise daily gratitude, you will see things that touch your heart everywhere. You will notice the little things that lift your vibration and make you feel so connected to life and nature.

If you want to focus on bird song in the morning, you will hear so much more than someone who hasn't set that filter. You will become attuned to the sounds of the different birds, the different tones, the calls, the layers upon layers of beautiful notes. It is magical. The empowering thing is, we get to decide what we focus on when we are conscious, when we choose to take our power back.

Coming back to expectation. In science, the hypotheses informs us of the expected result. Sometimes, something else happens other than the prediction. New inventions, creativity, they don't come from the known. If they came from the known, they wouldn't be new.

Our lens of perception gets coloured by what we are told, what we are programmed to believe, and our own life experiences. It will see the perceived outcome in its own unique way. Three people with the same task, will all expect different things. So how can we fail, when the concept of failure in itself comes from expectation? (Remember the quantum physicists and the particles.)

Expectation is a thought. A thought is not the truth, it

can change, so maybe failure isn't true? You might not have achieved your expected outcome, but isn't that the experiment of living and learning? It is feedback, it is an experience, it is gaining knowledge and wisdom. Thats where the magic is for me.

Delving into the power and the weakness of the mind a little more, I want to say that I love my own mind. It's sharp, it loves studying, looking at the world, analysing, it has enabled me to write this book, to structure my thoughts in a way that makes sense.

However, the thing that has caused me the most suffering in my life wasn't actually the physical cancer or surgeries. It was my mind. My expectations, and my thoughts that I believed to be the truth at the time. Thoughts create an emotional state, we feel the emotion, how we feel is how we experience our precious and beautiful lives.

During the trauma that my mind kept bringing me back to, I kept returning to the teachings that I had studied over the period of many years to cope. It is one thing to study a philosophy, it is another thing to live it, and to embody it. I returned to the yogic philosophy, and the buddhist and shamanic teachings that I love so much. I knew that the answers were inside of me, not outside. I kept sitting with myself, I did a lot of breath work, meditation, hatha, jivamukti and yin yoga.

My consistent practises, daily essential oil protocols and self inquiry were my medicine. They shone the light for me to see the way out of my suffering. I had just forgotten to embody it. I kept remembering that I was not my thoughts. That thoughts and emotions come and go, they feel intense, they peak, if I sit with them, be aware of them, give them some space and honour them, they subside. They can either pass completely, or if something needs to change I can take action to initiate that change. This was my remembrance.

Thoughts are not the universal truth, how can they be? They are our experience, our lens of perception, so if everyone in the world is viewing things differently where is the truth? It can't be felt in the mind. When I really got it, when I felt that permeate my whole body and my senses, I felt liberated.

I chose to keep returning to my heart, one moment at a time, to the peace that was always there, inside of me, as a steady constant. A peace that I could find anytime I chose to extract myself temporarily from my minds thoughts that were causing me pain and disrupting my inner calm.

With compassion for myself, I saw flashes of the version of me, that cared so deeply about what others thought of me, and wanted to comply with what others expectations of me were. An expectation, in essence is a thought. Thats all, a thought, nothing to feel pressured by. If we choose not to be.

I had been keeping myself in such a container of expectation. Not fully expressing who I am, or standing in all my unique weirdness. I am still de-conditioning from this to some extent. We are all taught to blend in, stay small, to consider what others think of us, and adapt our behaviour accordingly.

So now, if I have a desire or a goal that I would really love to achieve. I state it, then I let the expectation go. I have studied myself and with an expectation, I can get too focused, it sets my nervous system into a hyper alert state. It doesn't feel good to me, I feel wired, I forget to look after all the other parts of myself and life. I have learnt to take aligned action, with lots more creative fun and rest in between than I ever allowed myself before. I keep moving, being curious, trusting, and finding joy.

I also trust that my desire, what I think I want, might not always be the best thing for me. There might be something else for me. I know that life takes us on a journey full of twists, turns, detours and sometimes we encounter road blocks and have to turn back. It might not make sense at the time, but when you look back through conscious eyes, you can see the logic, you can see the journey clearly. The more I surrender expectation, the more fun, joy and amazing things that my finite brain could never have imagined, happen.

I really hope that this concept is one that you take with you, for the rest of your life. Your mind is finite, it can only know what it has experienced in this lifetime, with what has been manifested into reality already.

At the same time, we live in a quantum world, with infinite possibilities, that the mind cannot even begin to understand. New creations start in the quantum, they start with imagination, they are new, they are fresh, they haven't been done before. Once we have downloaded inspiration, the mind must then get involved and is super useful with the logistics, with the grounding of your idea into reality. But imagination is the spark.

Your mind is limited, you, as a soul are unlimited. So many things are possible that the mind will never be able to expect or guess. Isn't that amazing? Thats why I learnt to surrender. I surrender to the fact that anything is possible. I also surrender to the fact that I can't predict or control everything. It feels so good when you can truly let go, if even momentarily.

Life for me now, happens less in the mind, and more in the world around me, the space around me, in my body, in the interactions that I have, in my senses, in my relationships.

Imagine, if the sum of your moments, how much presence, how much joy, how much feedback you gained, how much love you felt, how much of your passion and purpose you stepped into, imagine a world that values that. Feel into the potential of a world that values wellness as a measure of success. Yes please.

If we return to the hypothesis, that we are all unique, and we are all here for a reason, to experience our lives in our own way, could not just living, being ourselves be the real success that we are aiming for?

The us before we got programmed and forgot our divinity, personal power and self worth. The us before we dimmed our light?

This is my aim in my life now, to strip back the layers that I have been hiding my light behind. To be me, fully, and unapologetically inside and out. In the process of rediscovering and living this, I aim to help as many people as I can do this too, by sharing my discoveries and holding space for them to see their own brilliance reflected back at them.

It is challenging to go against the 'norm,' as we are social and tribal creatures, we still have the caveman and cavewoman need to fit in, so that we aren't ejected from the tribe. It is a survival technique that was useful, but is not needed in our modern diverse global world. The small tribes that were needed to stick together to defend and live on the immediate land, to a large extent, have been absorbed into a global community.

So without this old structure, could we say that there is no normal anymore? That we give our power away when we desire to be normal, when we opt to dim our light, to hide our own blend of weird, to not honour our own or others uniqueness?

You are here beautiful soul, please be you, with no expectations from others.

Expectations aren't real, you are.

If we start to embody our uniqueness. If we begin to observe and believe that our own thoughts and opinions change in every moment, to consider the possibility that they are not true, how can they be met? How can anyone else's expectations of us ever be met? How can anyone else live up to our own expectations of them? They can't, as none of it is real.

It is powerful to have experiences, just for the sake of having experiences, and there is always something to be learnt, or to let go of during the experience, or after, upon reflection.

From an early age, I have always wanted to do a parachute jump to see how it felt. I did a tandem one for a charity, when I was in my busy, cram my life full of big experiences, scarcity phase.

I let go of the need to control everything, I experienced what it felt like to fly.

I learnt what it felt like to completely place my life in the hands of someone else, to surrender.

I learnt that when they span me around at the start of the jump, it looks great for the camera, but made me feel very sick.

I learnt that next time I would wear a face shield as I didn't like the sensation of not being able to catch my breath during the free fall part.

I learnt what freedom felt like on the other side of fear. I felt empowered. I literally felt like superwoman when I landed, like I could do anything I desired. Everything and anything felt possible.

Life for me is to be felt, a series of experiences, that

result from the choices that I make. I like to make my choices with a sense, of 'well what if,' and 'let's see'.

I test life.

I sample life.

I am curious, because I cannot possibly know it all and I certainly am not in control of it all.

Life is a bit like a practise for me, like my meditation practise and yoga practise. When I have perfected it, I will be an enlightened being. Until then I am practising. I am experimenting. I am aware that there could be a number of different outcomes. If we knew what the outcome would be, it wouldn't be an experiment.

This feels like freedom to me.

What people deem as failure, I see as feedback. I learn. I am sure you will have heard this analogy, but it is such a good reminder. Babies when they learn to walk or crawl, they keep going, they keep falling, we don't tell them that they have failed. We see them learn something each time, fall, adjust, try again.

When did that stop? When did it become expected to do things the first, second or third time that we try something new? When did we become so hard on ourselves?

When did life get so small that we couldn't have experiences just for the sake of it? Why does it have to lead to a desired outcome, can't it just be for fun?

A few years ago, I started applying this to my business and life. To have maximum fun, to do what lit me up, to study, apply, try, tweak, pivot, with no expectations. Since I have done this, I am making more of an impact in the world and I am so much happier.

I have stopped giving my power away to the constraints that life imposes. In my coaching, I have enabled others to see through their shadows and beliefs. I can do this because, I have personally done the work, and still am. Me first. Then I share. That is one of my mottos. I learn. I try. I embody. I share, whether it positively impacted me, or negatively. Without this authentic experience, I couldn't lead others towards their inner truth. I would just be teaching knowledge, not embodied wisdom.

An invitation, to start to free yourself from the concept of failure, to release imagined expectation, and give yourself complete permission to experiment, so that you can shine brighter with each bit of feedback you receive. So that you can share your wisdom with your loved ones and maybe a wider audience.

If it is resonating, if it sparking some deeper wisdom within you, if expectations aren't real, can you really fail? We have a desire, or a loose goal, a direction, but we know that things change, we can't predict anything, can we expect to be able to expect anything?

Some questions for you.

Have there been some things in your life, that you could

never have expected, but have been the most magical, special, life changing, or affirming experiences? List them in your journal or workbook, so that your brain can see proof that amazing things have happened to you that you could never have expected, predicted or controlled.

What has society programmed your reticular activating system to see, to think, to experience?

What have you at some level given your power away to?

<u>I don't fail</u>

I choose to experiment
I choose to play
I choose to try
I choose to learn
I choose joy
I choose to live

CHAPTER THIRTEEN
I LOOK UP TO THEM BECAUSE I DON'T FEEL ENOUGH

This was a big one for me. Mrs control freak, very much still in recovery. Mrs, I know best, I want to help everyone around me and keep them safe.

It was my study of yoga and the embodiment of it, that led me to uncover this way that I was giving my energy away, and also as a side effect taking others power away from them.

As we started to investigate in a previous chapter, we have this concept in society of 'looking up' to another. This is so damaging at the level of humanity.

At the core of my beliefs, we are the same, we are all pure light, we are all here for soul evolution. We are all at different stages, but all from the same source. All walking home, just on different paths, and some of us are a little further along on our own individual path in terms of our souls growth.

I am a 'wise old soul' I always have been in this incarnation, in this body. I feel things, I know things, I can sense things. Because I can feel how another is feeling, I have ideas and solutions come to me intuitively, and my ego wants to help. I used to talk over people sometimes in conversations, or interrupt. I was over flowing with good advice. I can remember feeling like I was literally going to burst if I didn't say it straight away, and was worried that I would forget what I was going to say. It came from a nurturing place, of wanting to make it better for them, wanting to nourish them. But, it wasn't helping anyone on any level. It was unsolicited advice.

Subconsciously, deep in my ego, I believed that I knew better than them. That I had the answers that they needed. That was so far from the truth. I was in reality, putting myself above them.

So now, if I do get some information through, which is still a lot. I bite my tongue, literally. If someone asks what I think, I will always share, but I won't say it's the way. I will ask how that feels to them. I will ask them what that would look like if they took that action? I would invite them to consider, how they think it would feel, and stress that this is my opinion at this moment in time, it doesn't mean that it is the way. It is my opinion from a thought, shaped by my lens of perception, that was created due to my programming and life experience. It is not the truth. It is not fact.

In the deconstructing of this belief towards others, this meant that no-one was above me. I had taken myself down from my own self made pedestal. Now for the hard bit, this meant that I was 'as good' as everyone else. Those souls that 'I looked up to,' the 'lucky' ones, the ones that had 'made it'. This was such a challenge for my ego. My putting myself above people was to help, this was another matter. I had to feel enough and gain self belief. I had to choose to decondition and reprogram.

In my studies and in my work as a healer and teacher at the time, I saw the beautiful limitless possibility in everyone

I was teaching, and was always so amazed that they couldn't see it in themselves. So, it was time to turn that observation inwards. I had a revelation that I share with my coaching clients and groups all the time. If I truly believe all that I have said above, that we all have limitless possibility, that no one is above the other, why am I so special? Why am I the only one that isn't enough? I must be so exceptional to be the only soul on earth who isn't enough? My ego literally could not argue with that! That limiting belief had no choice but to go. It still returns for a visit every now and then, until I smile and remember.

I'm not special.

We all are.

When we try and enforce our beliefs upon the other, when we try and steer and micro manage, we are inadvertently attempting to take their power away. We are teaching them that they must listen to guidance outside of themselves. We are attempting to take away the possibility of them getting things wildly 'wrong'. We are taking away growth, experimentation, and encouraging the status quo. We don't grow by just listening to, and following others advice. We grow by learning how to listen to ourselves, by trying out things that work and things that don't. We grow by learning to take sovereignty of our own lives.

At the core of looking up to others, we don't feel enough. Children are so beautiful as they do tend to naturally feel enough, they are born with the belief that anything is possible until it gets programmed out of them. They believe that they can be anything, and they don't see a problem in having whatever they want, at that very moment, hence the tantrums. Slowly, over time, the programming creeps in, resulting in the limits that bind us.

I wish with all my heart that you start to shine the light of awareness and remember that you are enough, you are whole, you are perfect and you matter. You are not more or less important than any other being on this planet. We have just been taught separation and polarity. We have had hierarchical systems imposed upon us. We have been brainwashed as to what is 'successful,' what is 'better than'. We have been taught to attach our worth and judge another's worth upon the labels and measures valued by our capitalist society. It feels like these concepts are stressed in our modern times, we are so polarised. It is time beautiful soul, to remember, to move away from this.

It feels like a lovely place to tell this story. As a still recovering control-aholic, I asked my husband to help with the easter bonnets one year as I was out teaching yoga the night that they needed to be made. My husband left early for work the next morning and when my daughter came down to breakfast she was in tears. The bonnet was horrendous, it was a brown papier mache lump. I truly always believe that there is a way, so foregoing breakfast, I got some easter decorations out, stuck and sellotaped them on and it looked cute. Away she went, with the motto, which she still quotes me on, "there is always a way."

The following year, I decided not to have to control it all, even after the previous years disaster. It was tough, but I was aware of myself. I was aware that it is exhausting to feel like I have to control everything. So I chose not to. I didn't want to live like that anymore. It is in these individual moments that we make change. It was a challenge, but I asked my husband to do the bonnet for my son, knowing also that I had some spare chicks and decorations just in case! The end result was such a beautiful and unexpected surprise the next morning. I was greeted with the most magical, creative monster head, it was amazing. Was it polished? No. But it was one of those imperfectly perfect creations with so much charm. I loved it. That creation would not have been born, if I was in control mode.

An invitation to reflect on all of this chapter and discover what your thoughts are.

I feel its absence

I hear all the time
You are enough
You are whole
You are perfectly imperfect
You are light
You are love

For a moment
My soul
The perfect imperfection
The light inside of me
Glimmers so brightly
I feel it

So bittersweet
To feel it for a second
So full of brilliance
Then to feel it go away
Back to living in it's absence
It hurts, I feel worse

I feel that small hopeful light inside of me
I can picture it trying so hard to grow bigger
Trying so hard not to go out
Trying to get some fuel
Some belief to keep the fire going

Life…words…rules…labels…comparison…
fear…I let them dim it

But, I know its there
I can't 'un-see' it

I can’t ‘un-feel’ it
I know it’s up to me
To start to fuel it

If only I believe …

CHAPTER FOURTEEN
FIGHTING CANCER

This is something that my heart really wanted to express from my own journey with cancer. I really hope that it helps you, if you have been journeying with it too, or helps you hold space for someone who is.

I have never felt comfortable with the concept of fighting cancer, like cancer is an enemy of mine.

In my logical but mystical mind, a cancer cell, is one of my own cells, that went rogue. That was either created to go that way, or had the potential to, and my lifestyle thoughts and actions activated it. Either way, it is me, I don't want to fight against myself. Fighting feels violent, it doesn't feel like a word I want to use when I am vulnerable and facing my mortality. Fighting also implies winning or losing.

For me, love, compassion and kindness are the energies I want around me, not the vibration of violence. Not the energy of all or nothing.

I began to investigate what I could do for myself. How can I nourish myself, how can I provide optimal conditions in my mind, my body, my environment to hold the space for my cells to not express themselves as cancer again? This feels more empowering to me. It was the start of my journey, that I share with you in this book. I believe that my thoughts affect how my cells express themselves (epigenetic's). I know that my actions, what I put into my body, the management of my emotions, how much sleep I get, how much movement, I get, all matter. There are so many things within my control that I can do to help myself.

Now, I am dedicated to myself. How beautiful is that? So beautiful I feel called to repeat it. Now, I am dedicated to myself. Does this sound beautiful to you, does it resonate, or does it provoke or trigger something within you, some conditioning?

With this devotion to self, I move towards soul nourishment and chasing joy. I gently unbind myself from my limiting beliefs. This is all a softening, whereas, fighting to me feels like sword upon sword, metal against metal. No resolution, unless one side gives up. Nourishing myself has a different energy.

I take radical responsibility for myself now, I haven't always.

It feels poignant to finally share a poem I wrote when I was 14 years old after my granddad Jack died. It feels like it is time for it to be seen.

Death

Naivety to death
A powerful and dangerous thing
Believing loved ones live forever
To leave your side
Never never
The only thing we are certain of
The powerful force of death

CHAPTER FIFTEEN
CELEBRATE YOURSELF...

As I am close to letting the world know about this book, I feel so called to share how I am feeling. As I type, I am shaking, my heart is hammering in my chest. One limiting belief after another keeps popping into my head, I am trying to not given them my attention, just a little nod and a smile. I am being triggered, massively, and I am relishing this chance to heal a pattern that keeps arising in my life.

This book has been written from my heart. As I edit the pages, and read the words, I can feel myself woven into it, my energy, my joy, my passion, my pain, my sadness. It is an expression of me. This feels very scary and vulnerable. In fact, it feels terrifying.

My old patterns which I adopted as a child because I did always feel different are arising, patterns of people pleasing, blending in, not being seen, not quite believing that I am an author, still a sense of not owning that yet.

My heart and my soul knows that I am an author, that I am a writer. Every time I say or think this, my tummy flips inside of my body, half excitement about stepping into my power and purpose, half nerves. It feels expansive. I am way past the edge of my comfort zone. I feel like I am inside that plane again just before my parachute jump.

Even though I can feel in my body and heart that I am on the correct path for myself, in this moment, my brain wants to keep me safe from the eyes of the world. Safe from judgements, safe from the comments of people who hold a different opinion to me. Safe from people who think that I believe that I am 'all that,' who might whisper or think to themselves, "who does she think she is to write a book, to share her opinion?" My ego wonders this about myself too sometimes.

I follow all of what I have shared in this book. I have also upped my self care practises. I am meditating more, using expansive daily essential oil protocols, reading, making the space for more yin yoga. I am off social media for a while, moving my body to sweat more, finally getting physio for a shoulder injury that has flared up, working outside as much as I can, turning my face towards the sun, to feel the light.

Remembering time after time, that my ego loves me and wants to keep me safe. But also remembering, that I love experimenting. I love being curious. I love sharing the things that help me with others, more than any vibration of fear that I hold in my body.

I am surrendering to my belief that we are all here to lift each other up, and I believe in my heart that some things that are contained in these pages, will help someone step into their own light, heal a little more and ripple this out to others.

I believe in me and I believe in this book.

I have been coaching an amazing writer who released her first book this year and is already mentoring aspiring writers. I asked her if she had celebrated her book, she hadn't. As I coached her, I asked about the possibility that it would be powerful to recognise what she had created, to celebrate and honour herself, her light and achievements. And to honour that energy that she has brought into the world.

I am at this stage now. My husband and friends are asking what I am going to do to celebrate. I have a pattern of achieving something, fist pumping the air when it is completed, feeling proud of myself for five minutes and then my ego asks, what next? I turn and start focusing upon a new project almost immediately.

This is a pattern that I wish to heal. It is something I see all around me. As I heal, as I step into my power, I know it will help others in my world.

I am going to slow down, I have placed other projects that I wanted to launch on hold. I am going to get curious and see what it feels like to celebrate myself and this creation for more than five minutes, however scary it feels.

I truly believe that when we feel resistance, that is where the soul lessons and healing are.

Behind the lack of wanting to celebrate, is fear. A fear of being seen, a fear of success, a fear of judgement, a fear of being labelled as arrogant and over confident. Because I have stopped judging others who celebrate their own successes and I advocate for it, it is time to give myself the same grace and encouragement.

Whether this book is a best seller, or whether it sells 100 copies, I have followed my heart. I have stepped into my passion, I have shared what heals me. I have written a book. That is a massive achievement.

I have taken daily consistent action to steady my nervous system, to dream the future version of myself who is an author. I have stretched my neuro-set point way beyond any sense of comfort. I have grown, I have changed, I will never be the same again.

I want to say thank you to, and honour the past versions of myself who brought me to this point, and the ancestors whose bones and experiences I stand upon. I feel called to honour and welcome in the future version of myself, the me that I am becoming, and the future versions of myself that I will keep stepping into. I have an intention for this period of celebration to be like a sacred initiation, into a new way of being and a new stage of my life.

My whole life will change the moment that this book becomes available to the world. I have no idea in what way, how could I? My brain is limited and I am unlimited.

But I am curious, I am open to the flow of where that action takes me. I know that it will be wonderful, it might be painful too. I will feel all sorts of feelings. I am sure I will get triggered and I will delight in it all.

So let's reverse engineer some of these fears and the things that I think people might say or think about me.

"Who do I think I am?" My answer, I am light, I am energy, I am a soul who is open and curious to life, experimenting, just seeing what it feels like to step into the possibility that I am a writer. I am shining my light so that those in my life who are ready, can step into theirs. I love myself, I am proud of myself and I do not want to keep putting myself down or hiding any aspects of my multifaceted, multidimensional soul anymore. I am here. I am standing in my power. Aaaah, it feels scary and amazing to write that.

"What if no-one buys my book?" I have changed so much writing this book, it doesn't matter to me. I mean that sincerely, I am creating this from my heart, with a sense of 'what if?' It has been an amazing experience, I have seen my own souls growth reflected back to me as I have written this book. I have cried, I have healed. That is priceless. If it becomes a best seller, that will feel amazing too. How I will feel? I have no idea, I will let you know.

"What will people think and say?" There is a saying that comes to mind, "what people think of me is none of my business." It really isn't. I cannot and will not take on the responsibility of everyone in the world's perceived reality. I will not be limited by it. Therefore, it is none of my business. I know that I will constantly be triggered and I will feel it all so deeply. However, with practise, I am confident, that I will be able to truly embody this, and with it so much healing and freedom will come to me.

My ego will tell me that I am not safe. My heart will remind me that I am safe. I will keep a mantra revolving around my head as a daily practise. I will repeat this time after time.

"I am safe.

I am safe.

I am safe."

I am choosing to partner with the fear that I hold, I am not denying it, together we will be brave, and I am so proud of myself for that.

So how will I celebrate? I am not sure yet, how exciting is that? I have written this to hold myself accountable, there is no where to hide, this chapter will make me celebrate. If you would like me to come and celebrate with you, to come and sign your book let me know. I would love to travel and meet the readers of this book.

A final point of contemplation for you, do you celebrate yourself?

From an end to a beginning

From an end to a beginning
That's the way it is
The never ending
Graceful flow of life
Interrupted by our ego's
Our delicate ego's
Our vulnerable ego's
Grasping onto what is
Turning our backs
On the endings
So full of pain and bliss
Rejecting change
In favour of stagnation
Protecting our hearts
From the fluctuations of
Letting go and letting in
Obsessed with the linear
We forsake the cycles of life
Our own as women
As humans
As souls
As beings on mother earth
Do you want a life
With only the known?
With nothing new?
Or do you hear the whispers of your soul
Singing sweetly in your ear
About magical new beginnings?
Be brave sweet soul
Let go
Gently let go
So you can move

With grace
From an ending
To a beginning
Thats where life is

CHAPTER SIXTEEN
FOR NOW…

Time to close the pages of this book for now. I hope that you return from time to time.

Thank you so much for spending this time with me.

I would love to hear from you. Let me know what thoughts, or changes this book invited into your way of being.

If you loved the book, it would really help me if you would leave a review please, and recommend this creation to anyone you feel would benefit.

What next? I have no idea. I am dedicated to flowing where my energy and joy naturally goes. This could be my only book, or the start of many.

I so wish for you, that you connect to your joy more, to that light that burns brightly inside of you.

Goodbye for now beautiful soul, thank you.

Sending Love K xxx

PS: If you feel called to work with me, you can visit my virtual soul space, it would be so lovely to connect and carry on the journey together. https://www.iamkarenjackson.co.uk

ENDNOTES

(1) Soulpreneurs are a rare breed of people that use their work as a way to express their higher self. They can be entrepreneurs, freelancers, healers, artists, coaches, etc. https://yourlightspace.co/2020/10/27/10-qualities-of-a-soulpreneur/

(2) From www.dictionary.com - whelm
to submerge; engulf, to overcome utterly; overwhelm, whelmed by misfortune.
verb (used without object), to roll or surge over something, as in becoming submerged.

(3) p25 p25 From the Cambridge dictionary online
overwhelm *verb* (EMOTION)
-to cause someone to feel sudden strong emotion:
-they were overwhelmed **with/by** grief when their baby died.
-I was overwhelmed by all the flowers and letters of support I received.
overwhelm *verb* (WATER)
-If water overwhelms a place, it covers it suddenly and completely:
-The water overwhelmed levees in the area.
-The rain that caused the flooding was of such unu

(4) Chi is the life force energy that is in the universe and runs through us, known in various systems as Ch, Ki, Prana. As an extra note, the gallbladder meridian is the place that anger and frustration moves through.

(5) https://www.health.harvard.edu/blog/is-crying-good-for-you-2021030122020

(6) https://blog.sciencemuseum.org.uk/rise-and-shine-daylight-saving-time-and-our-body-clocks/

(7) Gay Hendricks - The Big Leap

(8) https://iamsahararose.com

(9) Essentialism: The Disciplined Pursuit of Less - Greg McKeown

(10) Deb Erickson https://www.icaninstitute.com

(11) https://www.santoshayoga.co.uk/about-andrea/

(12) Asanas are the physical shapes and postures that a student makes in a yoga class and practise.

(13) Oxford Languages

deserve/dɪˈzəːv/verb: **deserve**; 3rd person present: **deserves**; past tense: **deserved**; past participle: **deserved**; gerund or present participle: **deserving** do something or have or show qualities worthy of (a reaction which rewards or punishes as appropriate)."the referee deserves a pat on the back"

(14) https://www.simplypsychology.org/maslow.html

(15) Oxford Languages

(16) Female **dictionaryhttps://www.ocf.berkeley.edu/**

(17) Oxford Languages

(18) better.com

ABOUT THE AUTHOR

Karen Jackson, born in Nottingham April 1974, still lives there. She had a few years away to study Law at University in London and a Masters in Human Rights and Civil Liberties.

Karen has always been a free spirit, deep thinker and the odd one out. She believes in living life, really deeply living life, especially since having cancer twice in her 30's.

She wrote and drew all the time as a child, it was her expression and still is. Karen finally found her voice and true expression at the grand age of 47. She finally started to believe that she was good enough, and that her inner wisdom and unique way of seeing things, are needed to be expressed in this World.

Karen writes to empower, to inspire, to help souls reconnect with their own uniqueness and to respect that in each other.

She holds the vision of a more peaceful and powerful collective, in touch with their own feelings, not the sanitised acceptable version of feelings that society encourages. True gritty, joyous, messy feelings, the feelings you feel when you are live consciously.

When Karen isn't writing, she is coaching her clients into their spiritual purpose in both life and business. Creating her podcast episodes, holding cacao ceremonies, nurturing her community of essential oil users, yin yoga students and magical UNBOUND members. Karen is multi-passionate, and also teaches shamanic journeying, the medicine wheel and creating abstract art. On top of all of this, she has a love of doing Human Design readings and has become one of the UK experts in this field.

Everything Karen devotes her energy to feels good for her, she has gone through the lessons that she shares in this book to discover her worth, to follow joy, to live.

Karen loves connecting.

You can find her SLOW DOWN Live Deeply Podcast on Spotify and Apple.

She is on instagram with the following handle @i_am_karenjackson

Her website is www.iamkarenjackson.co.uk

COPYRIGHT

BOOK DESCRIPTION

Overwhelmed is destined to be in your hands, if deep down in your soul, you know that there is more. That you are more. You long for a soul connection to life. You are ready to step into your own unique power. To come back home to you, to drop the masks that exhaust you.

It is for you if you have ever uttered these words and phrases.
"I am overwhelmed."
"I don't have time."
"I am busy."
"I can't."
"I should."
'I'm fine."

This is for you if you are tired of this society with all its expectations, perfectionism and pressure. Society likes our feelings nice and sanitised.

I'm here to guide you to discover the freedom inside of you. To become conscious of the words that you use. To heal, to make your life feel more spacious, to discover what you truly think and believe.

Time to take your power back.

We take a journey together, to spark your curiosity, to discover the words that take your power away. You learn to discover how you really feel, so that you can heal and live life in your unique power. This practical guide will help you come back home to you and all your feelings.

Learn to live and feel again.

Printed in Great Britain
by Amazon

11590803R10108